The LITTLE BIG
BOOK of
Pooh

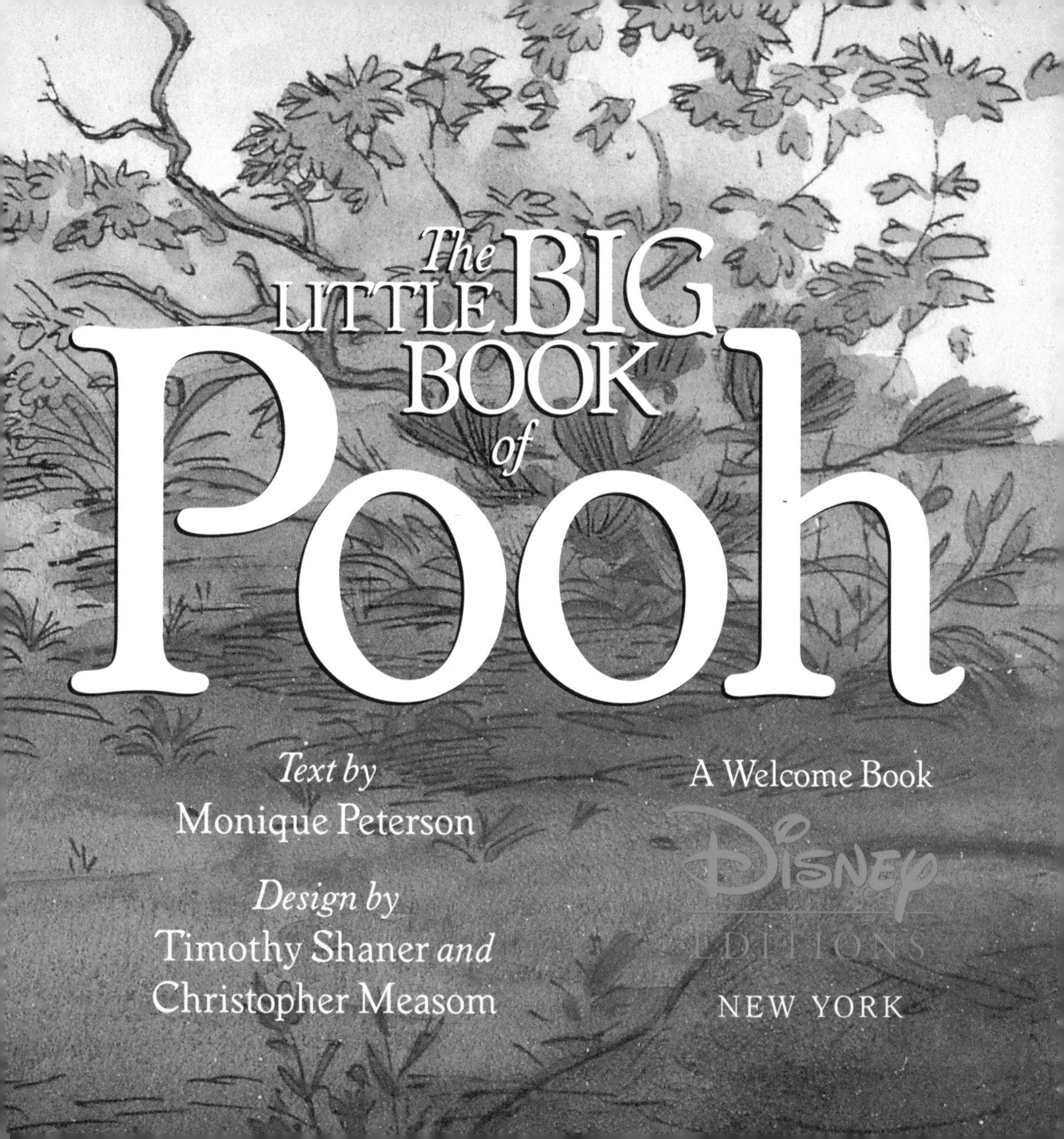

The LITTLE BIG BOOK of Pooh

Text by
Monique Peterson

Design by
Timothy Shaner *and*
Christopher Measom

A Welcome Book

DISNEP EDITIONS

NEW YORK

Copyright © 2002 by Disney Enterprises, Inc.
Additional copyright information on page 349.

Based on the "Winnie the Pooh" works, by A. A. Milne and E. H. Shepard

Academy Awards® and Oscar® are registered trademarks of the Academy
of Motion Picture Arts and Sciences.

Emmy Award® is a registered trademark of the National Academy of Television Arts & Sciences.

For information address:
Disney Editions
114 Fifth Avenue
New York, New York 10011

Editorial Director: Wendy Lefkon
Editor: Jody Revenson

Produced by:
Welcome Enterprises, Inc.
588 Broadway
New York, New York 10012

Project Director: Alice Wong
Project Assistant: Larry Chesler
Designers: Timothy Shaner
and Christopher Measom

Library of Congress Cataloging-in-Publication Data on file.
ISBN 0-7868-5364-6

Printed in Singapore

First Edition

10 9 8 7 6 5 4 3 2 1

CONTENTS

STUFF AND FLUFF

TIME FOR SOMETHING SWEET

AMUSEMENTS AND ACTIVITIES

IT'S A HUNDRED-ACRE WORLD

8

Introduction

Were it not for a father who cherished the adventures enacted by his young son at play, some might say Winnie the Pooh would never have been born. The story of Winnie the Pooh is that of an unlikely hero who started out as one child's plaything and became an international icon. Winnie was an actual bear, a gentle inhabitant of the London Zoo, who caught the fascination of both A. A. Milne and his son, Christopher Robin. The literary world of the Hundred-Acre Wood created by Milne came to life with the gift of a teddy bear, and a real forest in which the bear and his boy lived and played.

The genuineness found in the world of Winnie the Pooh has sparked the imaginations of adults and children since he first appeared in the pages of *Punch* magazine in 1924. Translated into dozens of languages, the stories communicate a common theme. Jeanne Lamb, director of the Central Children's Room at the Donnell Library Center in New York City, calls it *humanity*. As guardian of the original stuffed animals that belonged to Christopher Robin Milne, she has seen millions of people react with great emotion to the sight of the silly old bear and his friends. She can attest that no matter an individual's age or cultural background, the reader will find that the world of Winnie the Pooh resonates a basic truth.

This book celebrates the world of Pooh, real and imagined. Catch glimpses of people and places that have contributed and added to the lore. Uncover items that have been born out of Hundred-Acre mythology, from merchandise and theme park rides to international festivals and museum exhibitions. And step off the beaten path to find Pooh-inspired events, such as the annual Eeyore's Birthday Party in Austin, Texas, and the International Pooh Sticks Championships held by the Royal National Lifeboat Institution in England.

For such an age-old bear, it seems silly to think there could be anything new to say. Yet he is still on the frontlines of popularity, from news headlines in China to a continuing film career. For those who think they have seen it all, this book includes a rare look at some never-before-published art found in the vaults of the Walt Disney animation library and archives, from the artists who gave a distinctly British bear an American home. Consider this book a honeypot, if you will, of all things Pooh, for whenever the mood strikes for a little smackerel of something.

WINNIPEG WINNIE

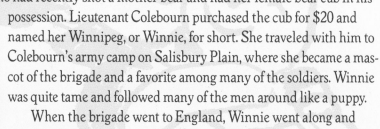

I f it weren't for a friendly bear at the London Zoo, Winnie the Pooh might still have been a Pooh, but he most likely wouldn't have been a Winnie. Christopher Robin's favorite bear owes his namesake to an American black bear cub discovered in Canada.

At the outbreak of war in 1914, English-born Lieutenant Harry Colebourn departed by train from his then-hometown of Winnipeg to join up with the 2nd Canadian Infantry Brigade. His train made a stop in White River, Ontario, where he met a hunter who had recently shot a mother bear and had her female bear cub in his

possession. Lieutenant Colebourn purchased the cub for $20 and named her Winnipeg, or Winnie, for short. She traveled with him to Colebourn's army camp on Salisbury Plain, where she became a mascot of the brigade and a favorite among many of the soldiers. Winnie was quite tame and followed many of the men around like a puppy.

When the brigade went to England, Winnie went along and stayed in Colebourn's tent. But by December of that year, his brigade was sent to France, and he needed to find a temporary home for Winnie. He made arrangements with the London Zoo to keep the bear on loan and visited her frequently when on leave. After the war, Colebourn returned to collect Winnie, only to discover that she had become extremely popular with the zoo's visitors. So, he permanently bequeathed Winnie to the zoo, where, in a few years' time, the young Christopher Robin Milne became a regular guest of the bear. Winnie lived at the London Zoo until her death in December 1934.

Introducing...
Mr. Edward Bear

February 13, 1924, *Punch* magazine published A. A. Milne's first account about the bear who "grows tubby without exercise." In the poem "Teddy Bear," our debut bear was neither a Winnie nor a Pooh. Rather, Teddy introduced himself to the king of France—and the public—as Mr. Edward Bear. (In England, Teddy is a nickname for Edward.) Most of his early adventures took place in Christopher Robin's nursery, where he spent time with books and toys, looking out the window, and falling off an ottoman. Later that year, Milne included "Teddy Bear" in *When We Were Very Young*, a collection of poems about Christopher Robin's friends. Edward Bear appeared twice more, but in picture only, not in name: at the top of the staircase and at the foot of Christopher Robin's bed. Within two years, Edward Bear confessed to Christopher Robin that he would like a more exciting name, and so, without a second thought, Christopher Robin christened his teddy Winnie the Pooh, and so he's stayed ever since.

WHEN WE WERE VERY YOUNG.

IX.—TEDDY BEAR.

A BEAR, however hard he tries,
Grows tubby without exercise.
Our Teddy Bear is short and fat,
Which is not to be wondered at;
He gets what exercise he can
By falling off the ottoman,
But generally seems to lack
The energy to clamber back.

Now tubbiness is just the thing
Which gets a fellow wondering;
And Teddy worried lots about
The fact that he was rather stout.
He thought: "If only I were thin!
But how does anyone begin?"
He thought: "It really isn't fair
To grudge me exercise and air."

For many weeks he pressed in vain
His nose against the window-pane,
And envied those who walked
about
Reducing their unwanted stout.
None of the people he could see
"Is quite" (he said) "as fat as me!"
Then, with a still more moving
sigh,
"I mean" (he said), "as fat as I!"

Now Teddy, as was only right,
Slept in the ottoman at night,
And with him crowded in as well
More animals than I can tell;

Not only these, but books and things,
Such as a kind relation brings,
Old tales of "Once upon a time,"
And history re-told in rhyme.

One night it happened that he
took
A peep at an old picture-book,
Wherein he came across by chance
The picture of a King of France
(A stoutish man), and, down below,
So,
These words : "King Louis So-and-
Nicknamed 'The Handsome.'"
There he sat,
And (think of it!) the man was fat!

Our bear rejoiced like anything
To read about this famous King,
*Nicknamed "The Handsome." There
he sat,*
And certainly the man was fat.
*Nicknamed "The Handsome." Not
a doubt*
The man was definitely stout.
Why then a bear (for all his tub)
Might yet be named "The Hand-
some Cub"?

"Might yet be named." Or did he
mean
That years ago he "might have
been"?

For now he felt a slight misgiving :
"Is Louis So-and-So still living?
Fashions in beauty have a way
Of altering from day to day;
Is 'Handsome Louis' with us yet?
Unfortunately I forget."

Next morning (nose to window-pane)
The doubt occurred to him again.
One question hammered in his head:
"Is he alive or is he dead?"
Thus nose to pane he pondered; but
The lattice-window, loosely shut,
Swung open. With one startled "Oh!"
Our Teddy disappeared below.

There happened to be passing by
A plump man with a twinkling eye,
Who, seeing Teddy in the street,
Raised him politely to his feet,
And murmured kindly in his ear
Soft words of comfort and of cheer :
"Well, well!" "Allow me!" "Not
at all."
"Tut-tut! A very nasty fall."

Our Teddy answered not a word;
It's doubtful if he even heard.
Our bear could only look and look:
The stout man in the picture-book!
That "handsome" King—could this
be he,
This man of adiposity?

"Impossible," he thought; "but
still,
No harm in asking. Yes, I will!"

"Are you," he said, "by any chance
His Majesty the King of France?"
The other answered, "I am that,"
Bowed stiffly and removed his hat;
Then said, "Excuse me," with an air,
"But is it Mr. Edward Bear?"
And Teddy, bending very low,
Replied politely, "Even so."

They stood beneath the window
there,
The King and Mr. Edward Bear,
And, handsome, if a trifle fat,
Talked carelessly of this and that . . .
Then said His Majesty, "Well, well,
I must get on," and rang the bell.
"Your bear, I think," he smiled.
"Good-day!"
And turned and went upon his way.

A bear, however hard he tries,
Grows tubby without exercise ;
Our Teddy Bear is short and fat,
Which is not to be wondered at.
But do you think it worries him
To know that he is far from slim?
No, just the other way about—
He's *proud* of being short and stout.

A. A. M.

POOH

or a bear of little brain, there is one thing Winnie the Pooh knows for certain: without fail, he can always tell when it's time for a little smackerel of something, which usually (and preferably) turns out to be honey. Pooh is also a master of disguise and has proved to be quite clever when it comes to fooling bees. A renowned explorer, Pooh has tracked some of the Hundred-Acre Wood's fiercer creatures—namely, heffalumps, woozles, and jagulars. He's also been as far as the North Pole. When he's not disguising himself in clever ways to trick bees out of their supply of honey, Pooh enjoys chasing butterflies, composing poetry, and spending time at his Thotful Spot.

EARS: Occasionally filled with small pieces of fluff, which often makes it difficult to understand what Rabbit is trying to say.

HEAD: Stuffed primarily with fluff; has little to no brain. Most often, Pooh's lack of brain doesn't pose a problem because his stomach does most of the thinking (see Stomach).

PAW: Exceptional dexterity as evidenced by tree-climbing skills and tossing Pooh Sticks. Serves dual function as scooper (good for honeypots and beehives).

STOMACH: Primary decision-making organ. Also contains special sonar (sometimes called "rumblies") that allows Pooh to detect as many as twelve pots of honey calling from his cupboard at once.

LEGS: Useful for scampering up trees and following in woozles' footsteps. Additionally (during times of being wedged in a great tightness), legs make excellent towel-horse or shelf holders.

"Winnie the Pooh"
Step-by-Step

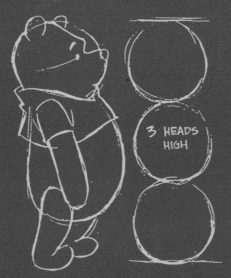

3 HEADS HIGH

EARS ANCHOR ½ WAY BETWEEN TOP AND BACK OF HEAD.

FACIAL FEATURES ARE ON THE FORWARD ⅓ OF HEAD.

EYE LINE

TOP OF MUZZLE SLIGHTLY ROUNDED

POOH HAS NO NECK.

SHIRT COVERS TOP ⅓ OF BODY.

COLOR SEP. ON BOTTOM OF FOOT WILL BE INKED.

LEGS ATTACH TO REAR ½ OF BODY.

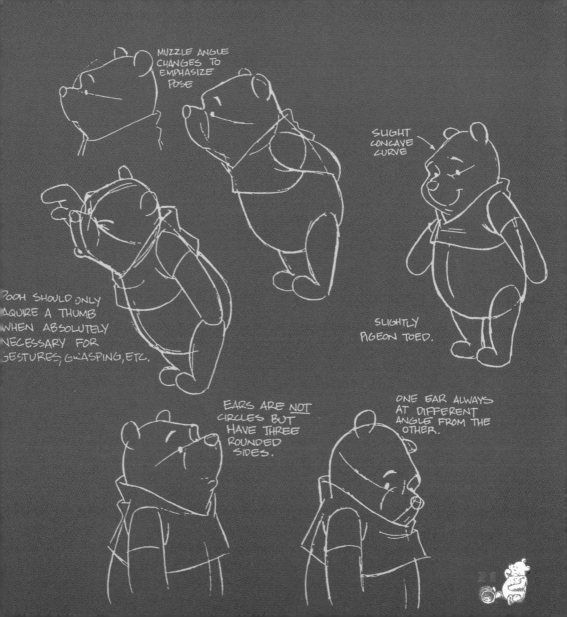

MUZZLE ANGLE
CHANGES TO
EMPHASIZE
POSE

SLIGHT
CONCAVE
CURVE

POOH SHOULD ONLY
ACQUIRE A THUMB
WHEN ABSOLUTELY
NECESSARY FOR
GESTURES, GRASPING, ETC.

SLIGHTLY
PIGEON TOED.

EARS ARE NOT
CIRCLES BUT
HAVE THREE
ROUNDED
SIDES.

ONE EAR ALWAYS
AT DIFFERENT
ANGLE FROM THE
OTHER.

Nom de Poohs

His common name is Winnie the Pooh, but to his friends in the Hundred-Acre Wood, he is so much more. For a little bear stuffed with fluff (and honey), adventures (and misadventures) have earned him many a nickname:

E. C. and T. F. (Eeyore's Comforter and Tail-find.

Very Wary Bear

P.D. (Pole Discoverer)   Pooh Bear   F.O. P (Friend of Piglet's)   Silly Old Be.

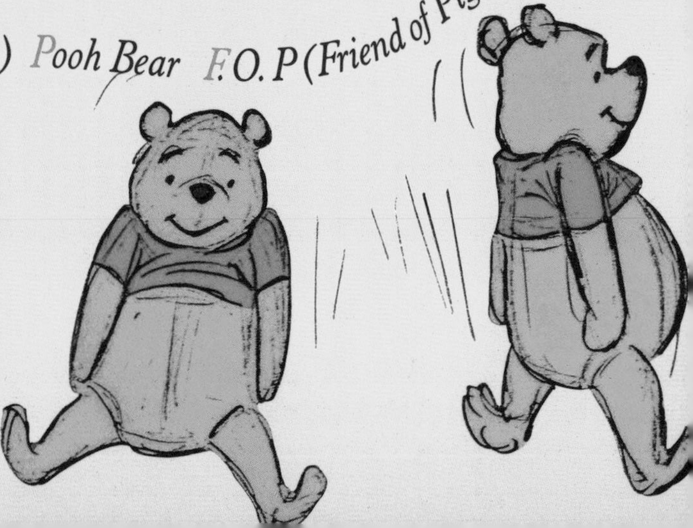

...ar of Very Little Brain Best Bear in All the World Brave and Clever Bear

...dward Bear Helping Bear Little Black Rain Cloud Sir Pooh de Bear

...bby Little Cubby R.C. (Rabbit's Companion)

Wedged Bear in a Great Tightness

23

A. A. Milne

Alan Alexander Milne had an early start at a literary life as the son of the headmaster of a private school called Henley House, where he began his education four months before his seventh birthday in 1888. While there, Milne received his early instruction and mentoring from the well-known writer, H. G. Wells. By the time he went to college at Cambridge University, Milne had become the editor of *Granta* and had his first humorous works published in *Punch* magazine, where he soon became a member of the editorial staff. *Punch* became a launching pad for many of Milne's essays, poems, stories, and plays, including his first child-centered stories about his niece, Marjorie.

In 1928, by which time Milne had written the collections for which he would be most remembered, he had already established his reputation as one of the foremost English humorists of his day—not as a children's writer. Milne admitted that he did not really know what a children's book was and

Right: Title page from Winnie-the-Pooh.

· A. A. MILNE ·

Winnie-the-Pooh

WITH DECORATIONS BY
ERNEST H. SHEPARD

PUFFIN BOOKS

originally intended the Pooh stories to be read by adults. Milne wrote his first children's book *Once On a Time* in 1914 for his and his wife's amusement "at a time when life was not very amusing." The story was filled with sophisticated humor and had its roots in a play he had written for British troops during the First World War. No matter who the intended audience may or may not have been, Milne was certain "that no one can write a book which children will like, unless he writes it for himself first."

Milne's children's books sold so well that Methuen, his British publisher, couldn't keep up with the sales and had continual difficulties getting enough paper to keep the stories in print. In 1941, Methuen explained in a letter to Milne that they could easily sell 1,000 copies of his "famous four" titles per week, but "we are rationed to under five hundred of each per week, and even then the binder sometimes lets us down."

Above: A. A. Milne, 1937.

Other Works by A. A. Milne

After Milne wrote his famous four—*When We Were Very Young*, *Winnie-the-Pooh*, *Now We Are Six*, and *The House at Pooh Corner*—he never wanted to write another children's book. He preferred being recognized as a playwright and considered his plays to be among his finest writings. Ironically, his fame would forever be connected to Winnie the Pooh, and many of his fans would never know he wrote more than thirty plays. His dramatic works include:

Ariadne
Before the Flood
Belinda
The Boy Comes Home
The Camberley Triangle
Charing Cross to Gloucester Road
The Dover Road
The Fourth Wall
Gentleman Unknown

The Great Broxopp
H for Helena: A Midsummer Night's Folly
The Ivory Door
The Lucky One
Make-Believe
The Man in the Bowler Hat
Michael and Mary
Miss Elizabeth Bennett
Miss Marlow at Play
Mr Pim Passes By
Other People's Lives
Portrait of a Gentleman in Slippers
The Red Feathers
The Romantic Age
Sara Simple
The Stepmother
Success
To Have the Honour
Toad of Toad Hall
The Truth about Blayds
The Ugly Duckling
Wurzel-Flummery

Left: A. A. Milne, 1948.

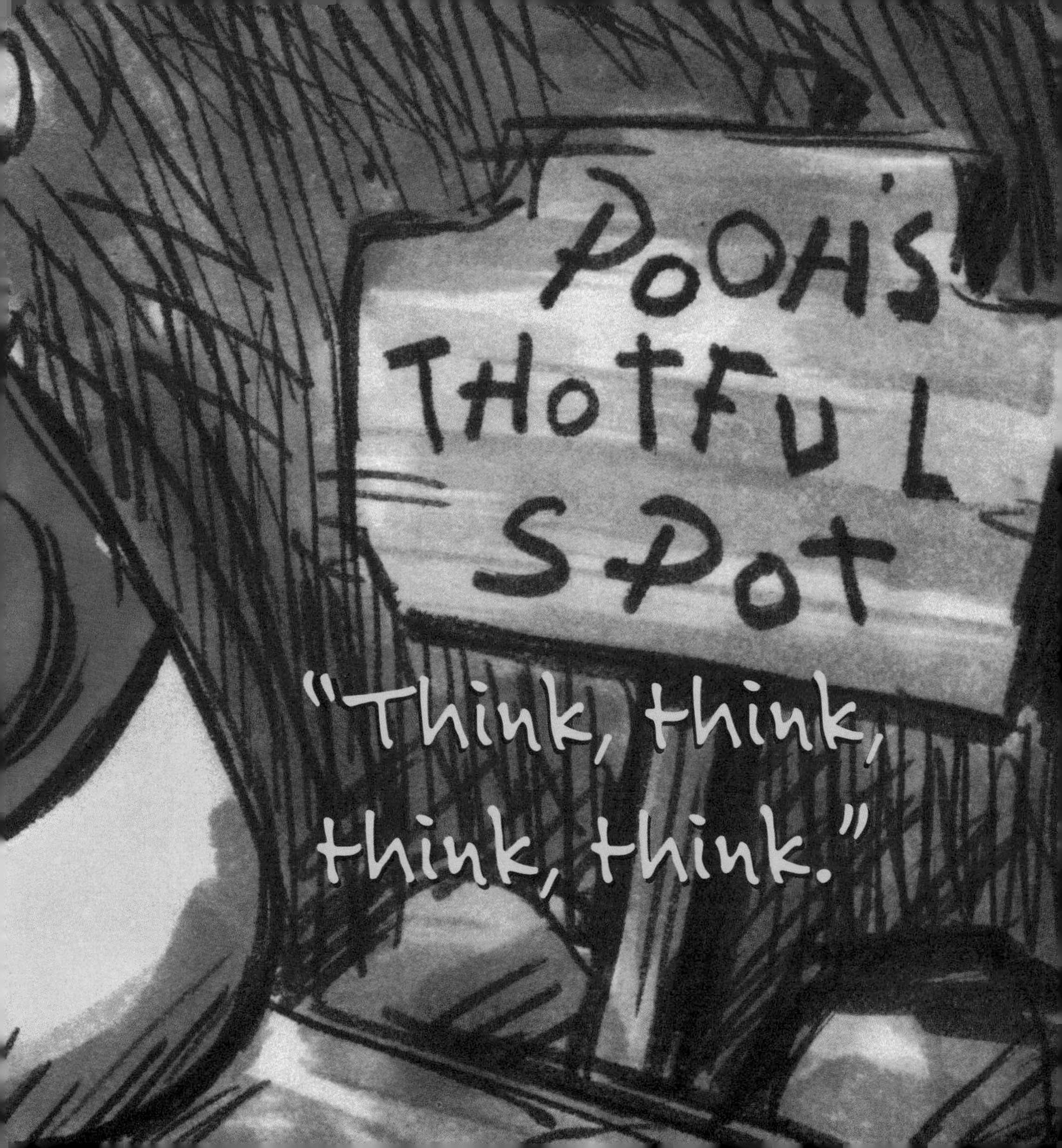

"Think, think, think, think."

Think, Think, Think

For a silly old bear, Winnie the Pooh has had many thoughts that don't really seem so silly at all...

On Expertise:
It takes a lot of honey-getting know-how to know how to get honey from a hive.

On Guarding Honey:
The safest place to keep honey from heffalumps is in one's tummy.

On Birthday Presents:
Nobody could be uncheered by a balloon.

On Memory:
If people are upset because you've forgotten something, console them by letting them know you didn't for-get—you just weren't remembering.

On Visiting Friends:
If someone takes a long time to answer the door when you knock, it may be because it's your own door.

On Getting Lost:
If you're looking for home, but keep finding a sandpit, try looking for a sandpit.

On Joy:
The way to stay the happiest is to let your tongue lickle and keep your tummy tickled!

On Doors:
It's important to have front doors that are big enough.

On Helping Others:
It's good to do small kindnesses for friends, such as pulling weeds in Rabbit's garden or trying to cheer up Eeyore.

On Knowledge:
What's wrong with knowing what you know now and not knowing what you don't know now until later?

On Size:
If bees were as big as heffalumps, they'd make an awful lot of honey.

Ernest H. Shepard

Ernest H. Shepard was born in 1879 and lived a mere five-minute walk from the birthplace of A. A. Milne. But it wouldn't be until after World War I, when they both had become members of the *Punch* editorial board, that they would meet and ultimately share linked fates.

Shepard's artistry grew out of the influence and instruction of his maternal grandfather who was a watercolorist. As a schoolboy, Shepard received his education in drawing and painting at St. Paul's school, which paid off later when he won a scholarship to the Royal Academy. At the outbreak of World War I, he served in the army, during which time he sent regular cartoons to *Punch*. Upon seeing some of these early illustrations, Milne commented to the art editor F. H. Townsend, "What on earth do you see in this man? He's perfectly hopeless." To which Townsend replied, "You wait."

Milne did just that, and before long, Shepard was providing drawings for Milne's countless poems and

Right: Ernest H. Shepard illustration from page 2 of Winnie-the-Pooh.

children's stories. By the mid-1920s, Shepard's popularity had grown immensely, and Milne asked him to provide new illustrations for previously published works, but Shepard, too busy, was unfortunately unable to fulfill all of Milne's requests.

One of the first questions Milne ever asked Shepard was whether or not he had read *The Wind in the Willows*, an accomplishment that Milne believed was a true test of character. Years later, Shepard would illustrate new editions of author Kenneth Grahame's very story.

Shepard remained an illustrator for *Punch* until his retirement in 1952. In addition to his world-famous Pooh illustrations, his classic line drawings can also be seen in Grahame's other works, *Dream Days* and *The Golden Age*, as well as one of Christopher Robin's personal favorite books by Richard Jefferies, *Bevis, the Story of a Boy*.

Above: Ernest H. Shepard, 1976.

33

The very first likeness of Winnie the Pooh appeared in the pages of *Punch* magazine in a cartoon by E. H. Shepard on November 26, 1913. Shepard's illustration of an anonymous bear sitting among other toys and stuffed animals was modeled after his son Graham's teddy named Growler. When the time came for Shepard to draw pictures of Christopher Robin's stuffed animal, Edward Bear, later known as Winnie the Pooh, he found that Christopher Robin's bear didn't have the same kind of tubbiness that he wanted for his honey-loving fictional counterpart. Growler, being a more portly teddy, became the perfect model for Pooh. Growler survived long enough to become the beloved, but worn, bear of Graham's daughter, Minette. Unfortunately, Growler met his fate in a Montreal garden when he came face-to-face with another growler— a Scottie dog.

GROWLER

Poohsticks Bridge

In 1907, Mr. Arthur Clough, resident of Hartfield village in East Sussex, England needed a more practical way to get timber to his estate on Cotchford Lane. So, thirteen men under the direction of Mr. Clough's estate manager, John Charles Osman, built a bridge that made travel possible between Posingford Wood and the estate on Crotchford Lane. The bridge, aptly named Posingford Bridge, became a permanent fixture of the larger wooded area known as Ashdown Forest.

Nearly twenty years later, Alan A. Milne and his wife Daphne purchased a farmhouse on the edge of Ashdown Forest from the earnings of Milne's first collection of poetry written for his son, Christopher Robin. The nearby woodlands became a fast favorite with young Christopher Robin and served

as the inspiration for *Winnie-the-Pooh* (1926), a collection of stories about Christopher Robin and his toys.

Although Milne transformed Ashdown Forest to the Hundred-Acre Wood in his stories, nearly all the stomping grounds of Pooh and his friends are based on real places: Eeyore's Gloomy Place, the North Pole, Galleon's Lap, Roo's Sandy Pit—and perhaps the single most popular landmark in the forest, the bridge where Pooh invented the game of Pooh Sticks.

Decades of horses, carts, and pedestrians eventually deemed the original Posingford Bridge impassable. Fortunately, by 1979, the bridge was fully restored and renamed Poohsticks Bridge. In 1999, the bridge once again needed to be completely rebuilt and was reopened to a welcoming public in January 2000.

Pooh Sticks players be warned: if ever your travels take you to Pooh's favorite bridge, plan to carry some sticks in your pockets. You'll be hard pressed to find any suitable twigs or branches nearby that haven't already been snatched up by the thousands of Pooh Sticks players who have gone there before you.

The Game of Pooh Sticks

For a game that requires quick-release dexterity of the index finger and thumb, a keen eye for fast-floating sticks, a certain amount of chance, and a willingness to let it all pass under the bridge, nothing compares to Pooh Sticks.

NECESSARY MATERIALS

Sticks (of varying length and width),
Bridge (preferably one that
accommodates pedestrians),
Running water (underneath the bridge),
Game partners (at least one!)

RULES OF PLAY

1. Find a stick.
2. Players should compare sticks to determine which stick belongs to whom. If necessary, mark the stick in a special way for easy identification.

3. Players should note which way the stream or river is flowing. Then, players should line up along the side of the bridge facing upstream. (*Hint: It's the side where the water flows* under *the bridge, not away from the bridge.*)

4. Players should hold out their sticks over the bridge railing, at equal heights above the water.

5. A designated player shouts, "On your mark ... Get set ... Go!"

6. Upon hearing the word "Go!" players *drop* their sticks into the water below. (*Note: Throwing is not allowed.*)

7. Players then rush to the other side of the bridge and watch to see whose stick comes out first. (*Cautionary note: Be mindful of other passersby on the bridge during this stage of the game.*)

8. The owner of the first stick that crosses under the bridge wins the round of Pooh Sticks.

9. Repeat for as many rounds as you like.

SPECIAL NOTE ON SKILL

Seasoned Pooh Sticks players know that winning is easier if you are able to master stick-dropping in a twitchy sort of way.

In the 1930s, Pooh Corner, a tea shop in Bristol, England, commissioned E. H. Shepard to do an oil painting of Winnie the Pooh holding his beloved pot of honey. The painting hung over the entranceway to the teahouse for many years until 1977, when Christie's of London put it up for auction and sold it for $4,400. Over the years, the painting changed hands and spent some time in Japan in a retrospective exhibition of Shepard's work.

On November 16, 2000, Sotheby's of London put Shepard's only known oil painting of Winnie the Pooh on the auction block. It sold for $240,000 to a group in Winnipeg called Partners in the Park, a volunteer board overseeing the management of the Pavilion Gallery Museum, the Leo Mol Sculpture Garden, and the Lyric Theatre (host of Winnipeg's annual Winnie the Pooh Friendship Festival).

Partners in the Park represented all donors who came forward to help in the initiative, including the government of Canada; the city of Winnipeg, Canada; the province of Manitoba; the Canadian Cultural Board; numerous corporations across Canada; and spirited individuals. Taking into account buyer's premium fees and taxes, the final cost of the painting totaled $274,853, the highest price paid to date for an image of the affable bear.

On June 3, 2001, Partners in the Park officially unveiled the painting to the people of Winnipeg and Manitoba on the steps of the Manitoba Legislative Building. Today, the painting hangs in the Pavilion Gallery Museum in Assiniboine Park as a reminder of the historical connection between Winnie the Pooh and the city of Winnipeg.

Portrait of a Young Bear

Billy Moon

On August 21, 1920, Alan Alexander and Daphne Milne signed the birth certificate of their newborn son with the name Christopher Robin. But they called him "Billy" from the start, and later "Billy Moon"— or simply "Moon"—inspired by their son's own pronunciation of his last name.

The first mention of Pooh came about in 1922 when Christopher Robin spent time feeding a swan at a lake near their summer cottage in Sussex. He called the swan "Pooh"—a good name, notes Milne in his introduction to *When We Were Very Young*, "because if you call him and he doesn't come . . . then you can pretend you were just saying 'Pooh!' to show how little you wanted him."

In January 1923, *Vanity Fair* published "Vespers," one of the first of several poems A. A. Milne wrote about his son. It would appear in the 1924 collection *When We Were Very Young*, which later became one of the best-selling books of its time. In that same collection, Christopher Robin's bear—

Right: Christopher Robin Milne, 1925. Center: Concept art for Winnie the Pooh and the Honey Tree.

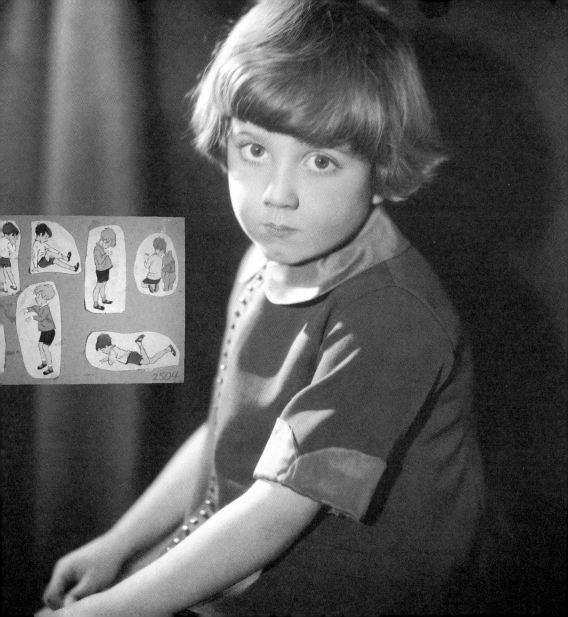

Billy Moon

not yet named Winnie the Pooh—made his debut in the poem, "Teddy Bear." The success of that book allowed the Milnes to afford a weekend retreat in the country near Ashdown Forest where Christopher Robin loved to play and climb trees—experiences that provided fodder for his father's poems and stories.

Christopher Robin's famous toy bear was a gift from his parents on the occasion of his first birthday. Eeyore arrived later that year for Christmas, and Piglet was a gift from a neighbor. The boy spent many hours creating improvised scenarios with his toys, which did not go unnoticed by his father. Poor Eeyore lost the stiffness in his neck rather quickly, giving him the rather gloomy appearance that established his disposition.

A. A. Milne relied so heavily on his son's playtime experiences for his writing, that when he needed new fictional characters, he purchased new toys for Christopher Robin,

Right: Christopher Robin Milne in his nursery, 1925.

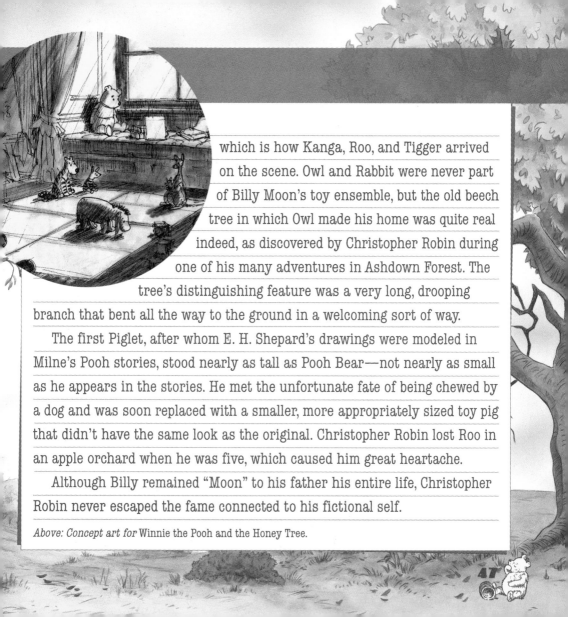

which is how Kanga, Roo, and Tigger arrived on the scene. Owl and Rabbit were never part of Billy Moon's toy ensemble, but the old beech tree in which Owl made his home was quite real indeed, as discovered by Christopher Robin during one of his many adventures in Ashdown Forest. The tree's distinguishing feature was a very long, drooping branch that bent all the way to the ground in a welcoming sort of way.

The first Piglet, after whom E. H. Shepard's drawings were modeled in Milne's Pooh stories, stood nearly as tall as Pooh Bear—not nearly as small as he appears in the stories. He met the unfortunate fate of being chewed by a dog and was soon replaced with a smaller, more appropriately sized toy pig that didn't have the same look as the original. Christopher Robin lost Roo in an apple orchard when he was five, which caused him great heartache.

Although Billy remained "Moon" to his father his entire life, Christopher Robin never escaped the fame connected to his fictional self.

Above: Concept art for Winnie the Pooh and the Honey Tree.

The Originals

As director of the Central Children's Room at the Donnell Library Center in New York, Jeanne Lamb always keeps a box of Kleenex handy in her office. Lamb sits within sight of the original toys that once belonged to the young Christopher Robin Milne. With approximately 750,000 visitors a year from all over the world who make the trek to see the fading animals, Lamb is prepared for a wide range of emotional responses. "We get a lot of older visitors—people who grew up in the twenties and thirties," she says. "When they see the animals, a flood of memories will come back."

But adults aren't the only ones wi~~~ ~~~led tears. "One or two kids will cry and say that's not Pooh," Lamb notes. "It's a difficult concept to get that this raggedy bear is the same as the one they see on the VCR at home."

From all of Pooh's visitors—old and young alike—Lamb hears one question more than any other: Why are the characters so popular? She offers her answer with a warm smile. "It's the stories," she says. "And how they treat each other. There's so much gentleness, caring, humor … the humanity of the stories resonates with all of us."

In 1947, Elliott Macrae, the president of E. P. Dutton, A. A. Milne's American publisher, arranged for the original Pooh, Kanga, Eeyore, Tigger, and Piglet to come to the United States for a ten-year tour, visiting the country's libraries and department stores. Fans flocked to see the stuffed animals and shared their enthusiasm in the guest book that traveled with the toys. A. A. Milne enjoyed reading the entries so much that he gave the toys to Macrae. The toys stayed with Dutton for forty years, until September 1987, when the publisher bequeathed them to the Donnell Library Center, where they

Guest-book entries from visitors from around the world:

"It's so good to finally see you!"

"Come home—all is forgiven."

"Happy to meet the original Tigger on my 48th birthday!"

"Our third visit. Couldn't go home without calling to see Pooh and friends."

"A lifetime ambition fulfilled!"

"Happy Birthday to me … a great way to celebrate!"

"The only reason for making honey is so I can eat it!"

Winnie the Pooh

and the Honey Tree

WINNIE THE POOH LIVES IN THIS enchanted forest under the name of "Mr. Sanders," which means he has the name over the door in gold letters and he lives under it. When Pooh hears his Pooh-Coo Clock, he knows it's time for something. So, being a bear of very little brain, he thought in the most thoughtful way he could think.

"Think, think, think. Oh yes, time for my stoutness exercise," said Pooh.

"Up, down, touch the ground," sang Pooh until he heard a little rumbling in his tummy. All that exercise made him hungry for a little smackerel of something.

So Pooh went over to his cupboard, took down his last honeypot, and stuck his nose inside.

"Oh bother, empty again—only the sticky part's left." Pooh couldn't believe his bad luck. Then all of a sudden he heard a familiar buzzing noise. "The only reason for making a buzzing noise that I know of is because you're a bee!" Pooh exclaimed happily.

And so Winnie the Pooh followed the bee to a tall oak tree and started to climb up to where other busy insects were buzzing around a hole in the trunk. He climbed and he climbed and he climbed. In his attempt to reach the delicious golden syrup, he entrusted his considerable weight to a much too slender bough. It snapped, and Pooh fell— "If only I hadn't . . . you see what I meant to do-oo-oo! And it all comes, I suppose, from liking honey so much! *OOF!* Oh bother!"—into a prickly gorse bush.

Pooh crawled out of the gorse bush, brushed the prickles from his nose, and began to think again. "Think, think, think." And the first person he thought of was his friend Christopher Robin.

Christopher Robin lived in another part of the forest where he could be near

Left: Winnie the Pooh lives under the name of
"Mr. Sanders." Cel setup.

his friends and help them with their problems. On this summer day, gloomy old Eeyore, being stuffed with sawdust, had lost his tail again.

"Eeyore, this won't hurt," said Christopher Robin.

"Never does," replied Eeyore. "It's not much of a tail, but I'm sort of attached to it."

Pooh interrupted the important task of pinning Eeyore's tail back, to ask if Christopher Robin had such a thing as a sky-blue balloon. "What do you want a balloon for?" asked Christopher Robin.

"Honey," whispered Pooh. "I shall fly like a bee—up to the honey tree, see."

So Christopher Robin gave Pooh a balloon. Then they went to a very muddy place, and Pooh rolled and rolled around until he was black all over. "There now, isn't this a clever disguise?" asked Pooh.

"What are you supposed to be?" asked a perplexed Christopher Robin.

"I'm a little black rain cloud, of course," answered the silly old bear. "Now would you aim me at the bees, please," instructed Pooh. So, disguised as a little black rain cloud, Pooh held onto the sky-blue balloon and floated up, up, up toward the scrumptious honey.

58

Right: Pooh climbs and climbs for something sweet. Concept art. Following pages: Christopher Robin helps Eeyore. Concept art.

"Eeyore, this won't hurt."

—CHRISTOPHER ROBIN

The bees were not entirely fooled by Pooh's disguise. They were, in fact, decidedly suspicious. But Pooh persisted: "Christopher Robin! I ... I think it would help with the deception if you would open your umbrella and say, 'Tut-tut ... it looks like rain.'" Christopher Robin went along with Pooh's plan, and this ruse actually permitted Pooh to come close enough to the honey to scoop a little into his mouth.

Unfortunately, the honey was laced with angry bees, which Pooh quickly spit out. "Oh! Christopher Robin! I have come to a very important decision. These are the wrong sorts of bees. Oof!" cried Pooh as the bees attacked Pooh and his balloon. The air quickly escaped from his balloon, and Pooh came tumbling down once more, this time toward Christopher Robin.

"I'll catch ... you, Pooh! Hurry, come on! The bees!" shouted Christopher Robin. With a swarm of vengeful bees in pursuit, Pooh and his friend escaped by diving into the mud-pool and taking shelter beneath the umbrella.

Above: "I'm a little black rain cloud, of course." Concept art. Right: "Christopher Robin, you can never tell with bees." Storyboard art.

Pooh was not the sort to give up easily. When he put his mind to honey, he stuck to it. Now honey rhymes with bunny, and bunny rhymes with ... "Rabbit!" thought Pooh. "I like Rabbit because he uses short, easy words like 'How about lunch?' and 'Help yourself, Pooh.'"

So Pooh decided to pay a visit to his friend Rabbit. But Rabbit was less than eager to have a hungry Pooh Bear visit at lunchtime and pretended not to be home.

"Bother," said Pooh. "Isn't there anybody here at all?"

"Nobody!" said a voice from inside Rabbit's house.

"Well, there must be somebody there because somebody must have said, 'Nobody.' Rabbit, isn't that you?" asked a confused Pooh.

"I don't think so," answered Rabbit. "It isn't meant to be." Knowing he couldn't hide himself from Pooh any longer, Rabbit opened the door. "Oh, oh hello, Pooh Bear. What a pleasant surprise. Uh ... how about lunch?"

"Oh thank you, Rabbit," said Pooh happily as he sat himself down at Rabbit's table and began helping himself to Rabbit's food.

"Would you like condensed milk or honey on your bread?" Rabbit offered, trying to be polite. Pooh tried to be polite, too, and asked for a small helping of both, but never mind the bread. However, when Rabbit gave Pooh the milk and honey, Pooh looked disappointed. "Is something wrong?" asked Rabbit.

"Well, I did mean a little larger small helping," admitted Pooh. So Rabbit gave Pooh the whole jar of honey, and Pooh ate and ate and ate and ate and ate and ate and ate and ate and ate. At last, Pooh said good-bye to Rabbit in a rather sticky voice. But when Pooh tried to make his way out Rabbit's door, he discovered his belly had become much too big. "Oh, oh, oh help and bother! I'm stuck!" cried Pooh.

Now Rabbit thought Pooh got stuck because he ate too much, but Pooh thought he got stuck because Rabbit's front door wasn't big enough. Whatever the reason, after much straining and struggling on Pooh's part, Rabbit realized there was only one thing to do—get Christopher Robin!

Above: "Never mind the bread, please. Just a small helping ...." Storyboard art.

While Rabbit ran off to get help, Pooh's friend Owl happened to pass by. "Splendid day to be up and about one's business, quite!" commented Owl. "Oh, I say, are you stuck?"

"No, no," Pooh answered quickly. "Just humming to myself—hum, hum, hum."

But Pooh's humminess was not convincing to Owl. "You, sir, are stuck. A bear wedged in a great tightness. In a word, irremovable. Now, obviously this situation calls for an expert."

Before Owl had a chance to say another word, Gopher popped out of his tunnel. "Somebody call for an excavation expert? I'm not in the book but I'm at your service. Gopher's the name—here's my card—what's your problem?" He whistled through his buck teeth.

Owl pointed a wing at the top half of Pooh. "It seems the entrance to Rabbit's domicile is impassable. To be exact—plugged!"

Gopher sized up the situation and determined that the first thing to do would be to get rid of the bear. "He's gumming up the whole project!" cried Gopher.

"Dash it all! He *is* the project!" insisted Owl.

So Gopher inspected the ground around Rabbit's door, above Pooh, below Pooh, and beside Pooh. "Um, hard diggin'... might hit bedrock... danger of cave-in ... risky ... needs planks for bracing," said Gopher. "Big job—could take two or three days!"

"Oh—blast it all!" exclaimed Owl.

"Good idea!" cried Gopher, excited about the possibilities. "We'll dynamite, save time! Well, I can't stand around lollygaggin' all day. I've got a tight schedule! Think it over and let me know. You got my card—I'm not in the book, y'know!" And as quickly as Gopher appeared, he dashed off, leaving Pooh just as stuck as before.

Soon, Rabbit returned with Christopher Robin and Eeyore. "Silly old bear," said Christopher Robin. "Here, give me your paw." He pulled and pulled, but it was no use. Pooh was still as stuck as ever. "Pooh Bear, there's only one thing we can do," Christopher Robin said solemnly. "Wait for you to get thin again."

"Oh bother," sighed Pooh. "How long will that take?"

Preceding pages: Rabbit might never be able to use his front door again. Concept art.
Above: Christopher Robin protects Pooh from bad weather. Cel setups.

"Days…weeks…months…who knows?" said Eeyore in his usual gloomy manner.

Meanwhile, Pooh's bottom half was causing Rabbit great distress. "Oh dear, if I have to face that, that thing for months…well, I might as well make the best of it," he lamented. So, Rabbit tried to turn Pooh's bottom into something decorative, yet useful. In no time, Rabbit put a picture frame around Pooh's bottom, set up a shelf across his legs, and for a splash of color, painted a big smiling face on Pooh's rear end. But something was still missing. Antlers! By placing a couple of branches in just the right spot, Rabbit succeeded in turning Pooh's bottom into a…moose shelf.

Poor Pooh had no idea what Rabbit was doing, but whatever it was, it sure did tickle. As he laughed and squirmed and squirmed and laughed, he messed up Rabbit's moose without knowing it. Just then, Kanga and Roo stopped by with a little surprise.

"Honeysuckle!" said Pooh with a big smile when he saw Roo's flowers. With a name like honeysuckle, Pooh figured the flowers were good enough to eat, and he sure was hungry.

But Kanga stopped Pooh before he could take a bite. "No, Pooh, you don't eat them—you smell them."

Right: Rabbit makes the best of it. Storyboard art.

"Oh," said Pooh, clearly disappointed. So, Pooh sniffed the honeysuckle, and as he did, he started to get that tickly feeling again. This time, it was in his nose. Meanwhile, Rabbit had just finished fixing up Pooh's backside once again when—"Ah…Ah…Ah-choo!"—all of Rabbit's Pooh decorations came crashing down on top of him.

While Pooh's bottom was stuck on the inside of Rabbit's house and his top was stuck on the outside of Rabbit's house, both ends waited to get thin again—day after day—night after lonely night. Pooh's thoughts kept drifting to food… to breakfast…and to lunch. One night, Pooh was dreaming of honey when Gopher showed up for the swing shift with his lunch box. "What sort of lunch is in that lunch box?" Pooh wanted to know.

"Well, let's see here," said Gopher as he pulled out the contents. "Summer squash, salmon salad, succotash, spiced custard…and honey!"

"Honey!" cried Pooh, smacking his lips. "Could you spare a small smackerel?"

Left: Helping Pooh pass the time. Concept art.
Above: "Hooray! Pooh will soon be free!" Cel setup.

But before Gopher could give Pooh one golden drop of delicious honey, Rabbit came running out and scooped Gopher's honey right out of his hands and posted a big sign that read, DON'T FEED THE BEAR!

Then one morning when Rabbit was beginning to think that he might never be able to use his front door again—it happened! Pooh budged. Rabbit was so excited he ran to tell Christopher Robin right away. "Hooray! Christopher Crabin...eh...oh...Christopher Raban...he bidged! He badged! He booged! Today is the day!"

So Christopher Robin grabbed Pooh's paws, and with the help of all their friends pulled with a heave...ho! Heave! Ho! H...E...A...V...V...V...E! They pulled Pooh with such a force that he sailed clear out of Rabbit's door up into the sky and straight into the top of a tall oak tree. But, this time, Pooh was in no hurry to be rescued, for he landed smack dab in the middle of a big, goopy glob of honey. "Yum, yum, yum," slurped Pooh. "Bears love honey and I'm a Pooh Bear...time for something sweet!"

Of all the happy endings to Pooh's adventures, this one was one of the happiest endings of them all. ■

Right: A happy ending—and time for something sweet. Concept art from Walt Disney Imagineering.

"Eleven-O'Clockish Honey Buns"

When it's time for a little smackerel of something, what could be better than the taste of milk and honey and bread … all rolled up into one sweet bun? Best served warm on a blustery day, just before an expedition, or to garner up a bit of courage to trap a heffalump.

For Buns:

1/4 -ounce package active dry yeast
1/4 warm water (100°F to 115°F)
1/4 cup honey
2 1/2 cups bread flour
1 teaspoon salt
2 large egg yolks
1/2 cup milk (room temperature)
1/2 stick (1/4 cup) unsalted butter, melted

For Glaze:

2 tablespoons honey
1/2 stick unsalted butter
2/3 cup confectioners' sugar

1. In the bowl of a standing electric mixer, sprinkle yeast over warm water and stir in 1/2 teaspoon honey. Let stand until foamy (about 5 minutes).
2. Gradually add remaining honey, flour, salt, egg yolks, and milk to yeast mixture and beat at low speed until blended. Add melted butter, and beat at medium speed until smooth (about 5 minutes).
3. Scrape dough from side of bowl. Cover. Let rise in warm, draft-free

place until dough has doubled in size (about 1 hour).

4. Prepare glaze. In small saucepan, heat glaze ingredients until butter is melted. Remove from heat and cover. Keep warm.

5. Punch dough down. Roll onto floured surface into 9" x 11" square and brush glaze on surface. Roll up dough lengthwise, jelly-roll style. Cut into 12 equal pieces and transfer to greased baking sheet. Brush more glaze on rolls. Cover and let rise in warm place until doubled in size (about 45 minutes).

6. Preheat oven to 350°F.

7. Heat remaining glaze and brush on rolls. Bake 15 to 20 minutes, or until golden. Transfer to wire racks to cool.

Makes 12 buns

POOH'S
THOTFUL
SPOT

The Buzz on Honey

HONEY. It is more than just Winnie the Pooh's favorite food. Long before our favorite bear discovered it in the woods, people were using honey as a natural sweetener, as a fundamental ingredient in medicinal remedies, and as the secret additive in cosmetics and skin care. Here are some of the bear essentials:

One tablespoon of honey contains 64 calories, 3.6 grams water, 8.1 grams fructose, 6.5 grams glucose, 1.5 grams maltose, 0.3 grams sucrose, 0 grams fat, 0 grams cholesterol, 0.6 milligrams sodium, 0.15 milligrams protein, and trace amounts of thiamine, riboflavin, niacin, pantothenic acid, vitamin B-6, folic acid, and vitamin C.

Did You Know?

In the world's oldest known surviving medical texts that date as far back as Egypt's Middle Kingdom around 1900 B.C., honey is the most popular ingredient in 500 out of 900 remedies for everything from the treatment of burns and open wounds to the care of sprains and fractures.

Mineral Rich!

Honey gets its minerals from the soil in which the pollen-giving plants are grown. Therefore, the mineral content of honey varies, but may include calcium, chromium, copper, iron, magnesium, manganese, phosphorus, potassium, selenium, and zinc.

Sweet Baking Tips

■ Honey is sweeter than sugar. When substituting honey for sugar in recipes, use 1 cup of honey for 1 1/4 cups sugar. ■ For cake and quick bread recipes, add 1/4 teaspoon baking soda for each cup of honey. This neutralizes the honey's acidity and allows the cake to rise properly. ■ Honey is approximately 17% water. Therefore, when substituting honey for sugar in a recipe, reduce the liquid content by 1/4 cup for each cup of honey used. ■ To prevent overbrowning when baking with honey, reduce the oven temperature by 25 degrees.

81

An Appetite for Fitness

He may be short and fat, but don't be fooled. Underneath that chubby, tubby stuff is one of the forest's fittest creatures. As a bear in the wild, he must hunt for his food, which is often a dangerous and strenuous activity. He keeps his strength up by sticking to high-energy food sources and eating smaller meals—frequently. He's very in tune with himself and knows exactly when he needs to replenish his body. Here's how Winnie the Pooh makes staying in shape and eating right seem as easy as doing nothing.

Start the day with a little stoutness exercise before breakfast.

Up…
down…
touch the ground!

Exercise should be enjoyable. You can easily prevent tubbiness by chasing butterflies, going on expotitions, or simply walking and humming. Climbing trees is also an excellent workout and well worth the effort if you choose a tree with a beehive in it.

When it comes to dieting, try to remember not to forget:

- You can always get thin if you wait long enough.

- If you don't have much of an appetite, a little up-down-touch-the-ground improves it right away.

- Keep a simple diet of natural foods (preferably fresh and straight from the source).

- Eat with friends.

- Eat small helpings. If your host offers you condensed milk or honey with your bread, just have the milk and honey.

Walt Disney's interest in adapting A. A. Milne's Pooh chronicles for animated films dated back as early as 1937, when he initiated a dialogue with Milne's agent, Curtis Brown, about obtaining the film rights to the stories. In 1938, Walt asked for a preliminary analysis of Milne's characters to help determine how they might translate to the new medium. The report recommended that Disney drop efforts to pursue rights for several reasons: none of the stories "contains anything even remotely resembling a plot," E. H. Shepard's whimsical drawings would be lost in animation, and any attempt to involve the Pooh characters in a longer story would kill whatever charm the books possess.

Nothing materialized at the time, and Disney looked into the matter again in the 1940s and 1950s. When Walt finally did acquire the rights to Pooh in 1961, he decided not to make a feature; rather he would test his audience with a 25-minute featurette. His rationale was that Winnie the Pooh was not a household name in the United States in the same way that it was in England, and he feared that the very British bear might not have the same appeal to American audiences. To complicate matters further, Pooh's world was a simple one, without the typical villains, plot twists, and resolutions that were common in so many of Disney's other films.

Above: Animator Hal King at the boards, 1965.

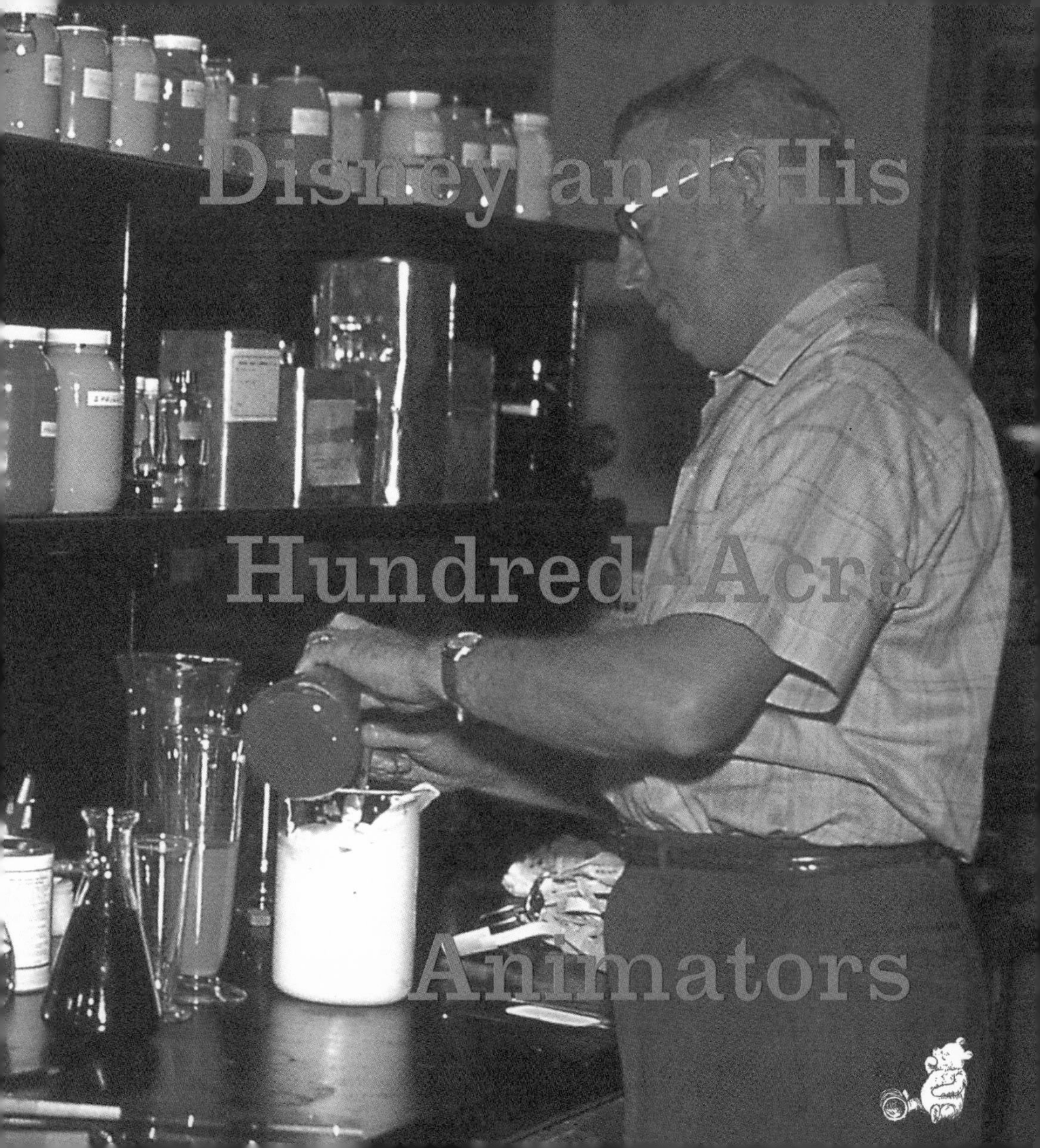

Adapting Milne's stories for the screen put Disney's animators to the test. E. H. Shepard's distinctive sketches posed the first problem. As animator Frank Thomas notes, "For animation you need a continuous outline. That's almost the opposite of the way Shepard gets his effects." The simple bear turned out to be the most difficult to animate, primarily because a teddy's movements are stiff and limited, as opposed to real-life animals like Owl and Rabbit.

By the time *Winnie the Pooh and Tigger Too* was in production, the challenges didn't get any easier. "There would always be something wrong," recalls animator John Pomeroy. Tigger "was going up too high or going down too low ... or the tail is too active. Everything had to be perfectly choreographed ... 'cause you never want to be aware that it's drawn."

Left: Animator Frank Thomas at the boards, 1968.
Above: Storyman and "Jack of all trades" Ken Anderson lends a hand, 1965.

Original Talents

Animators: Milt Kahl, Ollie Johnston, Frank Thomas, Eric Cleworth, Eric Larson, John Lounsbery, Art Stevens, John Sibley, Cliff Nordberg, Don Bluth, Walt Stanchfield, Hal King, Gary Goldman, Hal Ambro, Burny Mattinson, Dale Baer, John Pomeroy, Fred Hellmich, Chuck Williams, Bill Keil, Richard Sebast, Andrew Gaskill

Background artists: Art Riley, Al Dempster, Bill Layne, Ann Guenther

Layout Designs: Basil Davidovich, Don Griffith, Dale Barnhart, Joe Hale, Sylvia Roemer

To paint the characters on celluloid, the backgrounds and all other color effects in Walt Disney's *Winnie the Pooh and the Honey Tree* required more than 400 gallons of paint weighing nearly three tons—enough to dress the exteriors of more than 100 average-sized homes.

The Disney studio paint laboratory produced nearly 1,000 different hues to complete the production. In addition to using the standard colors that line the shelves of the typical paint dispensary, Disney ink and paint specialists created new shades like Pooh beige, Christopher Robin blue, Kanga brown, Piglet pink, and Eeyore gray.

Pooh's Hues

Not in the Book

The Hundred-Acre Wood engineer-geologist-miner who specializes in tunnel excavation, house fortification, and wall building may have rattled the foundation of Milne's classic stories for many a fan, but Disney was not the first to dream up the new character. When Walt Disney started plans to adapt A. A. Milne's stories for the screen, he felt that, along with the traditional characters, the picture called for a gopher. In order to appease die-hard Milne fans, every time the gopher appeared in the movie, he explained his presence by way of a sign or by calling out, "I'm not in the book, you know."

The press was mixed on the new addition. Some reviewers felt that had Milne included a gopher, it would have been very much like Disney's. Others bitterly criticized the impudence of Disney artists to tamper with the classics.

Milne's niece, Angela, however, couldn't see what all the fuss was about. In the British magazine *Punch*, she revealed that her uncle had actually planned to have a gopher in his stories. "He told me an odd story once about having seen a newspaper report about a curious animal that had escaped from an American freighter," she said of Milne. "It was a gopher. We don't have gophers in England, and he became fascinated with the creature and wrote several chapters about it." It was the British publisher who rejected the gopher segments of the Pooh stories, claiming that an animal indigenous to the North American continent wouldn't be keeping in style with the rest of the stories.

Gopher's Better Business Tips

- Buy bulk! (That's my motto.)

- Keep your productivity up and your overhead down.

- If it's not in your job specification, just say "No can do."

- If you must work on a holiday, be sure to charge two times time-and-a-half overtime.

- No charge accounts. Work strictly in cash!

- When in doubt about how to get a job done, blast it!

94

■ Always keep a
trade secret. I work
in volume.

■ When somebody calls
for an excavation expert,
just remember that the worst
thing in tunnel boring is losing your
tunnel bearings.

■ Always be mindful of efficiency: Don't waste
time lollygagging when it's time to get to work!

■ You don't have to be in the book to be available for service, you know!

Ashdown Forest Flora & Fauna

In the fourteenth century, Ashdown Forest in England was used as a hunting ground for royals, and was home to a variety of deer, including red deer, fallow, and roe, as well as boar, wolves, foxes, and Pine Martens. Today, it is the largest protected area of open land in southeast England. As one of Europe's few remaining expanses of lowland heath, Ashdown Forest supports a wide range of flora and fauna.

Although the land was much more forested during the years A. A. Milne and Christopher Robin spent significant time there, it is still recognizable today, with its varied woodland of birch, oak, willow and pine trees, as the place that gave inspiration to the Hundred-Acre Wood and the many adventures that took place there.

In addition to sheep, cows, and grazing ponies, Ashdown Forest shelters hares, hedgehogs, and owls. Here are some of the other lesser-known inhabitants of the wood:

Bracken

Wood lark

Fallow deer

Marsh gentian

Heather

Furze

Musk thistle

Silver-studded blue butterfly

Sand lizard

At Home *with* Rabbit

Every home decorator knows a house should match one's lifestyle. Being a woodland creature, Rabbit must constantly be prepared for all kinds of unexpected visitors. (He knows the importance of having a front door *and* a back door.) He is also a prudent gardener who harvests regularly prize-winning crops. Within his community, he is a true leader and must be able to accommodate large groups for entertaining or holding important meetings.

This country garden house is charming and cozy, yet organized, practical, and designed with the needs of the gardener in mind:

THE SINK and PANTRY: Organizing your kitchen pantry is a great way to get the clutter out of your life and make cooking and food preparation a snap! Display decorative canning jars from your annual harvest on open pine shelving for that added country look. Organize your pots and pans in a practical manner for efficiency and convenience. A

deep sink basin with an old-fashioned water pump is ideal—especially at harvesttime!

THE HEARTH: Nothing is more welcoming in cold weather months than a cozy fire in the hearth. Always keep a spare log ready to burn on dark nights or blustery days, in the event small and fearful neighbors drop in suddenly.

THE FLOOR: Hardwood floors can take the wear and tear of owl talons or donkey hooves. Large open spaces work well for impromptu gatherings.

THE WALL DECORATION: If some temporary obstruction blocks an entryway or light into your home, make the best of it. Decorate! An empty frame or old windowpane of the sort you can find at country yard sales will work wonders as wall ornamentation. Extra legs on the wall can serve as towel racks, or as a shelf support. Add a bit of cheeriness with a doily and flowerpot. Or, for a more rustic flair, hang a pair of antlers on the wall.

RABBIT'S DAY PLANNER

MONDAY

1. Call meeting about something important.

2. Weed garden. (Note to self: gardening should be fun!)

3. Clean up destruction from Tigger's bouncing.

THURSDAY

1. Sweep floor.

2. Get rid of bugs in garden once and for all!

3. Replenish month's honey supply after Pooh's visit.

4. Do yesterday's unfinished chores.

Must increase productivity by 200%!

FRIDAY

1. Find out what Christopher Robin has been up to in the mornings.

2. Plan today's surprise party for Eeyore. (Note: include list of things everyone should remember not to forget.)

3. Bake Eeyore's birthday cake.

TUESDAY

1. Organize an expedition to teach Tigger a lesson!

2. Air out house.

3. Do spring cleaning.

WEDNESDAY

1. Rake leaves.

2. Mop.

3. Visit friends.

4. Develop emergency plans for "Rabbit's Rock Remover!"

5. Oversee boulder removal from Eeyore's house!!

SATURDAY

1. Hoe garden.

2. Pick and peel beans.

3. Make bean soup.

4. Re-hoe garden after Gopher's tunnel-digging excavation through cabbage patch.

SUNDAY

1. Read "The Bunny's Farm Companion."

2. Relax. Make list of next week's activities.

THE IMPORTANCE OF BEING
R A B B I T

No other creature is capable of mustering unflappable import to the same degree as Rabbit. An expert at all things of great significance, Rabbit will hop at any and every opportunity to take charge and delegate tasks. As Rabbit knows better than anyone, being important means:

- Organizing things when no one else will (such as searches for small friends and relations).

- Writing notices like "Don't feed the Bear."

- Gathering public opinion.

- Being Captain.

- Being one of the few animals in Hundred-Acre Wood who can think.

- Calling meetings when something important is afoot.

- Saying, "Now," when overseeing the dropping of stones in the river to help wet donkeys come ashore.

- Making helpful presentations to instruct others, as in "Rabbit's Helpful Guide to Celebration Organization."

- Shouting, "Go!" during Pooh Sticks games.

- Keeping things in proper perspective— e.g., "Look at all the work we have to do!"

- Having enough discipline to stay behind and do work while others go off on an adventure.

- Having the foresight to come up with a plan (whether it be to remove a boulder, prepare a party, or lose a Tigger).

- Saying you know what you're doing.

- Being busy.

"I don't mind the leaves that are leaving. It's the leaves that are coming."

Winnie the Pooh

and the Blustery Day

ONE BRISK AUTUMN MORNING in the Hundred-Acre Wood, Winnie the Pooh discovered that the leaves had blown off all the trees in the night, and now the wind was trying to blow the branches off, too. On this blustery day, Pooh decided to visit his thoughtful spot. And on the way he made up a little hum. Fortunately, Pooh's thoughtful spot was in a sheltered place where he could sit down and think of something. So, Pooh sat down and tried to do just that: "Think, think, think, think, think." Nothing seemed to happen, so Pooh tried harder. "Think, think, think—"

Just then, Gopher popped up out of his hole. "Say ... what's wrong, sonny, got yourself a headache?" He whistled through his buck teeth.

"No," Pooh replied. "I was just thinking."

"If I were you," Gopher said, disappearing down his gopher hole, "I'd think about skedaddlin' out of here."

"Why?" asked Pooh, suddenly confused.

"'Cause it's Windsday!" echoed Gopher.

So Pooh followed Gopher's advice and skipped away. And as he did, the most wonderful thought came to him: "I think I shall wish everyone a happy Windsday," he said. "And I shall begin with my very dear friend Piglet."

Now, Piglet lived in the middle of the forest, in a very grand house in the middle of a beech tree. Piglet loved it very much, for it had been in the family a long, long time. The sign next to his house still bore the name of his grandfather, Trespassers Will, which is short for Trespassers William.

On this blustery day, the wind was giving Piglet a bit of a bother. Every time he swept the swirling leaves away from his doorstep, the wind would blow them right back. Then one particularly strong gust of wind blew a big leaf right under Piglet and swept him away! "I don't mind the leaves that are leaving," cried Piglet. "It's the leaves that are coming!" And as little Piglet tried to get back on his feet,

Right: The wind was giving Piglet a bit of a bother. Storyboard art.

the blustery wind blew him into his very good friend, Winnie the Pooh.

"Happy Windsay, Piglet," smiled Pooh.

Piglet struggled against another gust of wind. "Well," he squeaked, "it isn't very happy for—for me."

"Where are you going, Piglet?" Pooh asked, watching his friend float up, up, up, above his head. Pooh grabbed hold of Piglet's scarf just in time to keep him from blowing too far away.

"Pooh—oh, oh, oh, I'm unraveling!" cried Piglet, holding desperately onto his scarf, which was becoming less and less of a scarf and more and more of a piece of yarn. "Whoops!" Piglet barely caught on to the last bit of unraveled scarf.

Piglet hung on tight, flying through the air like a pink striped kite. As the blustery wind continued to blow Piglet through the sky, Piglet continued to pull Pooh through the woods until by and by they found themselves outside Kanga and Roo's house.

"Look, Mama, look," said Roo from his mother's pouch, "a kite!"

"Oh my goodness," said Kanga, "it's Piglet!"

The wind carried Piglet farther away. "Oh, dear, oh, de—de—de—de—dear, dear!" cried Piglet as Pooh skidded with him. Soon they found themselves blowing

Right: Eeyore surveys the wreckage Pooh and Piglet leave behind. Storyboard art.

through Eeyore's Gloomy Place, where Eeyore was putting the last brace on his lean-to. Eeyore could hardly believe his eyes when Pooh skidded smack-dab into his house and clobbered it to pieces.

"Thanks for noticing me," Eeyore said, looking dolefully at the wreckage.

But Pooh couldn't stop to help. He was being dragged through Rabbit's garden, digging up all of Rabbit's precious carrots with his heels. Then the wind blew so hard that it scooped Pooh off his feet and sent both him and Piglet all the way through the Hundred-Acre Wood. Soon, they came upon Owl's house. Owl had been dozing away in his rocking chair, when—*BANG!*—Piglet smashed into his window.

"Whoo?" said Owl, fluttering open his big eyes. "Whoo, whoo, who is it?"

"It's me," Piglet called helplessly. "P-p-p-p-please, may I come in?"

"Well, I say now," said Owl with wide eyes. "Someone has pasted Piglet on my window." Suddenly, with an "Ooh!" Pooh smashed into the window next to Piglet. "Well, well, Pooh, too," Owl chuckled. "Do come in and make yourselves comfortable." Owl opened the window and in blew Piglet, Pooh, and several leaves.

"Happy Windsday, Owl." said Pooh.

"Ho, ho, ho, ho! My good fellow," Owl hooted. "I wouldn't go so far as to call it Windsday. Just a gentle spring zephyr." As Owl rocked back and forth in his rocking chair, his house rocked back and forth in the wind, sending Owl's table—and the honeypot resting on top—sliding across the room toward Pooh and Piglet.

"Excuse me, Owl, but is there honey in that pot?" Pooh asked.

"Oh yes, yes, of course—help yourself," said Owl.

Pooh stretched an eager paw for a little smackerel of honey, but the wind blew the honeypot out of reach. Soon, Pooh and Piglet were sailing across the room, but Owl was too busy with his story to notice. "Now, as I was saying, this is a mild spring zephyr, compared to the big wind of Sixty-seven ... or was it Seventy-six? Oh well, no matter—oh, I remember the big blow well."

Owl droned on, oblivious to his toppling china cabinet, shattering dishes, and tumbling furniture, until suddenly—*CRASH!* His entire tree house fell to the ground.

Preceding pages: A rather blustery day in the Hundred-Acre Wood. Storyboard art.
Left: Pooh and Piglet pay Owl a surprise visit. Storyboard art.

Now, as soon as Christopher Robin heard of the disaster, he hurried to the scene of Owl's misfortune. "Owl, I don't think we will ever be able to fix it." Christopher Robin said when he saw how badly Owl's house was damaged.

"If you ask me," said Eeyore, who'd just arrived, "when a house looks like that, it's time to find another one. Might take a day or two," moaned Eeyore in his usual gloomy way, "but I'll find a new one." And without another word, Eeyore strolled off in search of a new home for Owl.

"Good," Owl said, reclining into his rocking chair, "that will just give me time to tell you about my Uncle Clyde...." Owl chattered away until the blustery day turned into a blustery night.

To Pooh it was a very anxious sort of a night, filled with anxious sorts of noises.

"*R-rower!*"

Pooh bolted up in bed. He picked up his popgun, tiptoed to the door, and opened it just a crack. Immediately, something sprang into Pooh's house and bounced Pooh flat on his back.

"*Rower!* Name's Tigger. T-I-double-Guh-Rrr. That spells Tigger. And I'm the only one!"

Right: "Hello, out there. Oh I hope nobody answers."
Storyboard art.

"Then what's that over there?" said Pooh pointing to the orange stripedy beast in the mirror.

"Huh? Oh, hey, hey, look, look, look," gasped Tigger, scrutinizing his reflection. "What a strange-looking creature. Hmm—look at those beady little eyes and that pur-posti-rus chin... and those ridickerous striped pajamas."

"Looks like another Tigger to me," said Pooh.

"Oh no, it's not," Tigger denied. "I'm the only Tigger. Watch me scare the stripes offa this impostor. *Rower!* Oh..." Tigger made such a scary face that he ducked for cover under Pooh's table. "Is—is—is—is he gone?" Tigger stammered.

"All except the tail," said Pooh, looking in the mirror. Tigger's tail zipped underneath the table and disappeared from view. "He's gone," Pooh assured him. "You can come out now, Tigger. Tigger?" And before Pooh knew what had happened, he was bounced flat on his back, nose to nose with Tigger.

Preceding pages: An anxious night for Pooh. Storyboard art.
Right: "Rower! Hello, I'm Tigger." Storyboard art.

"I'm hungry!" announced Tigger.

Pooh cast an anxious glance toward his honeypot. "Oh not for honey, I hope," he fretted.

"That's what Tiggers like best!" cried Tigger as he helped himself to a big mouthful of delicious sticky goo when, suddenly: "*Yecch!*" Tigger gagged. "Tiggers don't like honey! That icky, stucky stuff is only fit for heffalumps and woozles."

"Well—well, what do heff-ah-oh-hall-laff-uh, what do they do?" asked Pooh.

"Oh, nothing much," Tigger replied casually. "Just steal honey."

Pooh grabbed his honeypot. "Steal honey?" he asked nervously.

"Yeah, they sure do," said Tigger. "Well, I'd better be bouncing along now … cheerio—oh—ho-ho-ho-o!" And with that, Tigger bounced away into the night.

Well, if what Tigger said was true, and there really were heffalumps and woozles about, there was only one thing to do—take drastic precautions to protect his precious honey. And so Pooh propped his popgun on his shoulder and guarded his stockpile with all his might. Now, the very blustery night turned into a very rainy night, and Pooh kept his lonely vigil hour after hour after hour until at last he fell fast asleep and began to dream.

Left: Pooh fell asleep and began to dream. Concept art from Walt Disney Imagineering.

In his dream, Pooh's honeypots warned him about the most horrible heffalumps and weasely woozles! The fierce creatures came in all shapes and sizes—square and round, up and down, checkered, striped, and spotted. Pooh tried to save his honey from the greedy, guzzling trunks of the heffalumps and woozles, but they multiplied and multiplied, and haunted Pooh the entire night.

When Pooh finally awoke from his nightmare, he found himself knee-deep in water. It was raining all over the Hundred-Acre Wood. It rained and it rained and it rained! The river crept so high out of its bed that it crept right into Piglet's house! Trembling with fear, poor Piglet floated all the way to his desk and scribbled an important message: "HELP P-P-PIGLET (ME)" He stuffed the note into a bottle, and tossed it out the window into the rushing current. Then Piglet started bailing. He bailed and bailed, and before he knew it, he was sailing atop his chair, bailing his way out the window.

Meanwhile, Pooh was desperately trying to rescue his supper and had lined up all his honeypots on a tree limb. Now that Pooh was stuck on the branch with nothing but honey, he decided it must be time for

Left and Right: Pooh tries to hang on to his honey.
Storyboard art (left), film still (right).

125

a little something. So, he poked his head into a very deep pot and slurped up so much honey that he nearly fell in. But as he sopped up his supper with his feet kicking in the air—*SPLASH!*—the river sopped up Pooh. He had toppled headfirst off the tree branch and directly into the churning waters below.

The Hundred-Acre Wood got floodier and floodier, but the water couldn't come up to Christopher Robin's house so that's where everyone was gathering. In the midst of all the excitement, Eeyore stuck stubbornly to his task of house-hunting for Owl. "There's one," Eeyore noted, eyeing the house floating past him down the river. "Cozy cottage. Nice location. Bit damp for Owl, though."

Meanwhile, little Roo made an important discovery. "Look," he told Christopher Robin, "I've rescued a bottle, and it's got something in it, too."

Christopher Robin pulled the note out of the bottle. "It's a message!" he exclaimed. "And it says 'HELP P-P-PIGLET (ME)'" Christopher Robin knew just what to do. "Owl!" he cried. "You fly over to Piglet's house and tell him we'll make a rescue."

Owl flew out over the flood, and he soon spotted two tiny objects below him. One was little Piglet, caught in a whirlpool, and the

other was Pooh, trying to get the last bit of honey
from the pot. Owl picked the closest perching spot,
which happened to be Pooh's bottom.

"Piglet, chin up and all that sort of thing!" Owl
reassured. "A rescue is being thought of . . . be
brave, little Piglet."

"It's awfully hard to be b-b-brave when you're
such a small animal," Piglet reminded him.

"Then, to divert your small mind from your unfortunate predicament, I shall
tell you an amusing anecdote," Owl proclaimed. So, Owl began another story and
he didn't notice Piglet trying frantically to get his attention. "I beg your pardon,
Owl," Piglet finally cut in, "but I th-th-th-think we're coming to a flutterfall, a
flatterfall, a . . . a wa-wa—a very big waterfall!"

In the very next moment, Piglet tumbled over the waterfall's edge with
Pooh—and the honeypot—tumbling after. The two friends plummeted down,
down, down, until they plopped into the pool below. Owl joined them just as
Pooh emerged, sitting on top of Piglet's chair. They floated to the riverbank where
Christopher Robin and the others were rushing to meet them.

Christopher Robin picked up his beloved bear. "Pooh! Thank goodness you're safe!" he cried. "Have you seen Piglet?"

"Excuse me," echoed Piglet's voice from deep inside the floating honeypot, "I have—oh what I mean is," said Piglet, popping out of the pot, "here I am!"

"Pooh," cheered Christopher Robin. "You rescued Piglet! You are a hero. And as soon as the flood is over, I shall give you a hero party."

And so, once the flood ended, the party began. Everyone was gathered around Christopher Robin's table, shouting cheers and hurrahs when Christopher Robin announced: "Attention, everybody. Now, this is a hero party, because of what someone did, and that someone is—"

Someone else cleared his throat, interrupting Christopher Robin's speech. It was Eeyore. "I found it," he said.

"Found what, Eeyore?" asked Christopher Robin.

"House for Owl," replied Eeyore. "If you wanna follow me," he said, sauntering off, "I'll show it to you."

So, everyone followed Eeyore. Then to the surprise of all, Eeyore stopped right in front of ... Piglet's house!

Christopher Robin was so flabbergasted and embarrassed that he couldn't think of the right words. Finally, he said: "It *is* a nice house, Eeyore, but...."

Kanga tried to help. "It is a lovely house, Eeyore," she offered, "but, but...."

Crushed, Piglet fought back tears. "It's the best house in the whole world!" he lamented.

"Tell them it's your house, Piglet," Pooh whispered.

Piglet shook his head. "No, Pooh," he sighed. "This house belongs to our very good friend—Owl."

"But, Piglet!" Rabbit protested. "Where will you live?"

"Well," Piglet sniffled. "I-I-I-I guess I shall live-ah—I-I- suppose I—I shall live..."

"With me," said Pooh, taking Piglet's hand. "You shall live with me, won't you, Piglet?"

"With you? Oh, thank you, Pooh Bear!" cried a teary-eyed Piglet. "Of course, I will."

Right: Everybody gathers at Christopher Robin's. Storyboard art.

"Piglet, that was a very grand thing to do," said Christopher Robin.

Rabbit, deeply moved by Piglet's gesture, agreed. "A heroic thing to do!"

Suddenly, Pooh had a thought. "Christopher Robin?" he asked, "Can you make a one-hero party into a two-hero party?"

Christopher Robin knelt down on the ground next to his friend. "Of course we can, silly old bear," he said.

And so Pooh was a hero for saving Piglet, and Piglet was a hero for giving Owl his grand home in the beech tree. Christopher Robin, Kanga, Rabbit, and Eeyore all celebrated by tossing Pooh and Piglet high in the air, cheering "Hip, hip, hooray, Hip, hip, hooray, hip, hip hooray, for Winnie the Pooh..."

And Piglet too! ■

Right: Hundred-Acre Wood celebration. Storyboard art.

"NOT MUCH OF A HOUSE, JUST RIGHT FOR NOT MUCH OF A DONKEY"

The day Eeyore builds himself a house in the story, "In Which a House Is Built at Pooh Corner for Eeyore," from A. A. Milne's *The House at Pooh Corner*, it disappears. On this very snowy day, Pooh and Piglet decide to do the seemingly roofless Eeyore a good deed by making him a house themselves. Unknowingly, they take the sticks from Eeyore's new home by his little woods and use them for their construction by Pooh Corner. When Eeyore finally finds his newer home, he agrees that it is better than his old home, but, sadly, it is not destined to last. Eeyore's home has continued to see destruction and reconstruction on a regular basis.

"Easy come, easy go."

"Might leak some, could be a bit drafty, sorta lopsided, kinda cramped . . . otherwise a dream house."

Happy Windsday!

Make the most of the next blustery day and organize a kite-flying expedition! Simple diamond kites are easy to make and respond well to gentle breezes. Lightweight materials work best, as Piglet knows from personal experience. *His tip:* if you don't have kite string, yarn from an unraveled scarf works exceptionally well.

MATERIALS:

3' x 4 1/2' sheet colored construction paper, two lightweight wooden dowels (36" and 54"), 2"-wide ribbon or fluorescent surveyor's tape, glue, kite string, scissors

TO MAKE THE FRAME:

1. Cut 1/8-inch deep notches at the ends of both dowels.
2. Make a cross with the dowels, centering the shorter stick about eighteen inches from the top of the longer stick. Tie them together with string.
3. Measure a piece of string long enough to stretch around the kite frame.
4. Tie a knot in one end of the string to anchor it in the top

notch. Thread the string through all four notches, creating a diamond shape. Wrap the end of the string around the first notch again and make a final knot. Make sure the string is taut around the frame.

TO ATTACH THE SAIL:

5. Set the frame on the paper and trim the paper to leave a one-inch margin around the frame. Cut away the corners.

6. Fold paper edges over the string frame and glue in place. Make sure the paper is taut.

TO MAKE THE BRIDLE:

7. Cut a piece of string the length of two sides of the frame. Tie one end at top of the spine (the largest dowel). Make a loop about one-third of the way down the string and knot it. Secure the end of the string at the base of the spine (the largest dowel) with a knot.

TO ATTACH THE TAIL:

8. Measure and cut a piece of string about five times the length of your kite.

9. Cut several 3-inch strips of ribbon and tie them onto the tail string, spacing them six inches apart

10. Tie the tail to the bottom spine (the largest dowel) of your kite.

11. Tie kite line to the bridle loop, catch a good wind, and your kite is ready to soar!

PIGLET

Piglet is considered one of the Hundred-Acre Wood's very small animals. He makes his home in a beech tree in the heart of the forest where his grandfather Trespassers William once lived, as evidenced by the signpost outside his door. Timid and easily frightened, Piglet prefers to stay safe and sound—far away from woozles, dangerous situations, or dark and stormy nights.

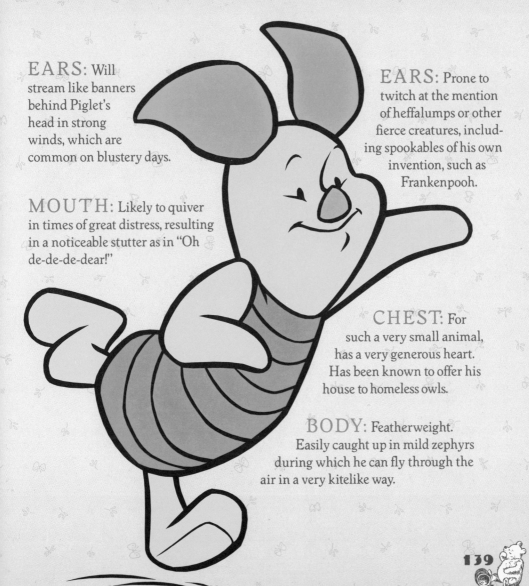

EARS: Will stream like banners behind Piglet's head in strong winds, which are common on blustery days.

MOUTH: Likely to quiver in times of great distress, resulting in a noticeable stutter as in "Oh de-de-de-dear!"

EARS: Prone to twitch at the mention of heffalumps or other fierce creatures, including spookables of his own invention, such as Frankenpooh.

CHEST: For such a very small animal, has a very generous heart. Has been known to offer his house to homeless owls.

BODY: Featherweight. Easily caught up in mild zephyrs during which he can fly through the air in a very kitelike way.

EARS ATTACH BETWEEN TOP AND SIDE OF HEAD.

PIGLET'S NOSE IS 3 SIDED YET ALMOST ROUND. LIKE THIS...

NOT LIKE THIS...

"PIGLET"
Step-by-Step

PIGLET IS PEANUT SHAPED

LEGS ATTACH TO UNDERSIDE OF BODY

2½ HEADS HIGH

STRIPES ARE
CIRCLES THAT
WRAP AROUND
BODY.

STRIPES ARE
IRREGULARLY
SPACED

NUMBER
OF STRIPES
CAN VARY FROM
9 TO 12.

Extra!

Kellogg to Make Cereals Based on Disney Characters

THE NEW YORK TIMES, Sept. 5, 2001— Pass the honey, please. Starting in 2002, Winnie the Pooh and his Disney pals will be a regular part of the breakfast roundup. The Walt Disney Company has granted the Kellogg Company exclusive rights to market breakfast cereals, Pop-Tarts, and Eggo Waffles based on Disney characters.

Disney Buys the Rights to Winnie the Pooh

THE NEW YORK TIMES, March 5, 2001— The Walt Disney Company bought the rights to Winnie the Pooh until the copyright expires in 2026. The sale marks Great Britain's largest literary contract to date. Beneficiaries include the Royal Literary Society, the Westminster School, and the Garrick Club.

Winnie the Pooh's Weight Alerts Agents

THE DENVER POST, Sept. 30, 2000— A suspiciously portly Winnie the Pooh bear led federal agents to detain two women on an Amtrak train in Albuquerque, New Mexico. The stuffed animal the women were carrying weighed a hefty 7.4 pounds, a considerable gain from Pooh's normal 2.5 pounds. Upon inspection, agents discovered $68,000 in cash hidden inside the bear.

"Pooh" Is on College List

THE NEW YORK TIMES, June 6, 2000— Winnie the Pooh may be a bear of little brain, but he's clearly stuffed with the right kind of fluff to make the grade. University of California at Berkeley faculty members have added A. A. Milne's *Complete Tales of Winnie the Pooh* to the recommended reading list for all freshmen.

Extra!

143

Extra!

A Wire-Filled Winnie the Pooh Goes Interactive

CHICAGO TRIBUNE, Dec. 3, 1998— Mattel Media has developed a huggable Microsoft product: a computer toy called My Interactive Pooh. Stuffed with wires instead of the usual fluff, this Winnie the Pooh doll can call a child by name, interact with a computer via cable link, and ask your tots whether they'd like to hear one of more than one hundred stories or thirty songs.

Winnie the Pooh Buyout Promises Struggling Writers a Taste of Honey

THE GUARDIAN, Aug. 7, 1998— With the proposed sale of the last twenty-seven years of copyright for A. A. Milne's Winnie the Pooh stories to the Disney organization, a honey of a windfall is expected for the British writers' charity, the Royal Literary Fund. The fund, one of the Milne estate's beneficiaries, has been providing monetary assistance to struggling authors for more than 200 years. Writers in the past who have benefited from the fund included Samuel Coleridge, Joseph Conrad, D. H. Lawrence, and James Joyce.

Fresh Stock to Revive Pooh-Mania

SOUTH CHINA MORNING POST, July 7, 1998— A fresh wave of Winnie the Pooh-mania is set to break out at 38 McDonald's restaurants where a new shipment of the toys will be available from July 24 to 28. Only one character will be offered each day of the promotion with a strict limit of one per customer. Latecomers for the first promotion broke down in tears, says McDonald's manager Catherine Chan Wai-ching. "We couldn't stand the crying, so we lied to them that they could get one later. Little did we know the lies were true." Proceeds from the sales are expected to net $2.5 million for the Ronald McDonald House in Sha Tin.

Pooh Fans Swarm Like Bees 'Round a Honey Pot

SOUTH CHINA MORNING POST, June 19, 1998— One hundred forty-three McDonald's restaurants were under siege yesterday after one million Winnie the Pooh toys in pajamas—costing $18 with purchase—were snapped up within a few days of a five-week promotion. Many of the stores have run out of stock, leaving collectors frantic and switchboards jammed. Some parents refused to leave the stores until managers opened new boxes of toys earmarked for sale in July. No longer able to satisfy the demand for the toys, marketing executives pulled TV advertising.

Pooh Gets His Day

NEWSDAY, May 5, 1998— New York City Mayor Rudolph Giuliani declared May 4 a citywide "Winnie the Pooh Day" as part of an ongoing effort to keep Pooh at his current home in the Donnell branch of the New York Public Library. The date marks the eleventh anniversary of Pooh's arrival to the library.

Tempest in a Honey Pot

SAN FRANCISCO CHRONICLE, Feb. 9, 1998— The Pooh Five will stay in New York, despite attempts by British Member of Parliament Gwyneth Dunwoody to demand the stuffed animals' return to their homeland. After a recent visit to New York, MP Dunwoody declared that Winnie the Pooh, Kanga, Eeyore, Tigger, and Piglet "looked very unhappy indeed." The issue became moot, however, after Prime Minister Tony Blair issued a statement supporting New York's stewardship of the world-famous dolls.

Don't Pooh-Pooh Pooh

ARTNET NEWS, July 21, 1997— Two E. H. Shepard pen-and-ink drawings sold for an overwhelming £67,500 each at a recent auction at Christie's London. The sketches, *I'm Not Throwing It, I'm Dropping It* and *Just the House for Owl, Don't You Think So, Little Pooh?*, went for more than four times their presale estimates. In all, 13 Shepard Winnie-the-Pooh illustrations sold for more than £205,000.

Canada Salutes Native Bear

BUFFALO NEWS, Nov. 3, 1996— Canada Post has released four commemorative stamps heralding Winnie the Pooh and his Canadian roots. The original Winnie was a female black bear cub purchased by Canadian Army Lt. Harry Colebourn during World War I. The 45-cent stamps show Colebourn with his beloved cub, Christopher Robin with his teddy bear, E. H. Shepard renditions of Pooh and his Hundred-Acre pals, and Disney's Pooh with Cinderella Castle at Walt Disney World in the background. The stamps were designed under the direction of Anthony Van Bruggen of the Walt Disney Company, Canada.

Extra!

In October of 1972 and 1976, Disneyland celebrated the national elections by hosting Winnie the Pooh for President Days. While on the campaign trail, the world's furriest presidential nominee could be found greeting guests and pressing paw throughout his Magic Kingdom "constituency."

Japan

Czech Republic

Sweden

Russia

International Bear o:

Since the birth of the world's most lovable bear in 1924, Winnie the Pooh has been translated into more than three dozen languages across the globe, including shorthand, Morse, and braille. Here's a sampling of Pooh worldwide:

- Winnie-die-Poeh (Afrikaans)
- Medo Winnie zvani Pooh (Croatian)

- Winnie de Poeh (Dutch)
- Winnie-La-Pu (Esperanto)
- Karu-Poec Puhh (Estonian)
- Palli Pumm (Faroese)
- Winnie l'Ourson (French)
- Poo Hadov (Hebrew)
- Bangsimon (Icelandic)
- Winnie Puh (Italian)
- Kuma-no-Puu-san (Japanese)

Norway

Poland

Finland

China

No) Mystery

- ■ Winnie ille Pu (Latin)
- ■ Miké Púkuotukas (Lithuanian)
- ■ Winnie Puff (Portuguese)
- ■ Winnie Ursuletul (Romanian)
- ■ Macko Pu (Slovak)
- ■ Medved Pu (Slovene)
- ■ Winny de Puh (Spanish)
- ■ Vini-der-Pu (Yiddish)

Hungary

Israel

149

How to Make a Trap for Heffalumps*

One cannot capture heffalumps or fiercer creatures without having a cunning trap. If and when the time comes for such a dangerous operation, there are a few important guidelines worth following:

*(or any of the fiercer creatures)

The first course of action is *deciding* to catch a heffalump.

Scout out the appropriate place to make a trap. Preferably, the trap should be somewhere near where the heffalump is, but about one foot farther away.

Dig a very deep pit. Be careful that the heffalump doesn't suspect what you're doing. *(Warning: make sure not to dig so deep that you can't get out when finished.)*

Put a jar of honey in the trap.

For best results, test the honey (to be certain that it doesn't just *look* like honey).

Go home and wait for the heffalump to come along and fall into the pit. Of course, it will be helpful if the heffalump is humming a little song, looking up at the sky, and wondering if it will rain.

In the morning, run to the very deep pit and check your honey to see if a heffalump has eaten it. It might help to taste the honey. (*Warning: if your head gets stuck in the jar, be careful that you don't get mistaken for a heffalump by your best friend.*)

In Case of Emergency

In the event you find yourself outwitted by the heffalump trapped at the bottom of a very deep pit for Poohs, just hum as if you were waiting for something. You may successfully unsettle the heffalump by telling him that you have fallen in a trap for heffalumps, then simply go on with your humming.

EXHIBITIONS

&

EXCURSIONS

When one little bear and his friends have warmed the hearts of so many people around the world for nearly a century, it comes as no surprise that these beloved characters should become a treasured subject of many a museum, display, and expedition. For true Pooh aficionados, here are places to see original artwork, enchanted places, and Hundred-Acre rarities:

■ **White River Heritage Museum, 200 Elgin Street, White River, Ontario, Canada** Visit the hometown of Winnipeg, the black cub who became the namesake of Christopher Robin's favorite teddy. Learn the story of how a young bear cub became a friend to many on both sides of the Atlantic, see rare Winnie the Pooh items on display, and check out the Pooh souvenirs.

■ **Donnell Library Center, New York Public Library, 20 West 53 Street, New York, New York, United States** See Christopher Robin's original stuffed animals that inspired the stories by A. A. Milne. Tattered and worn by years of love, Pooh, Piglet, Tigger, Kanga, and Eeyore remain on permanent display behind glass at the library.

■ **Pooh Explores, 22 Warleigh Road, Brighton, East Sussex, England** Take a guided walk through Ashdown Forest and visit the original Poohsticks Bridge, Eeyore's Gloomy Place, Roo's Sandy Pit, and other wonderful places that inspired the Hundred-Acre Wood stories. Led by Twentieth Century Walks, the tours take place Saturdays in July and August.

■ **Victoria and Albert Museum, Cromwell Road, South Kensington, London, England** See E. H. Shepard's original drawings and sketches, including those that first appeared in *Punch* magazine and the publications *When We Were Very Young, Winnie-the-Pooh, The House at Pooh Corner,* and *Now We Are Six.* In total, ten volumes of Shepard's work reside in the museum's print room.

W.T. Pooh p 133

■ **Pooh Corner, High Street, Hartfield, East Sussex, England** Visit the very shop that Christopher Robin and his nanny went to every week for bull's-eye candies. The 300-year-old Queen Anne–style shop has been specializing in "Pooh-phernalia" since 1978, and boasts the largest selection of Pooh-related merchandise in the world.

■ **The British Library, 96 Euston Road, St. Pancras, London, England** Take a peek at four rare plasticine models of Tigger, Roo, and two Poohs that E. H. Shepard created for his friend, Harry Stopes-Roe. The figurines, all less than three inches tall, are accompanied by a letter written by Shepard in Pooh's handwriting and spelling. The letter is a reply to Stopes-Roe's invitation to a party, which Shepard and Pooh were unable to attend, and includes a drawing of a weeping Pooh Bear.

TIGGER

igger's enthusiasm and natural bounciness
has rattled, shaken, frightened, and even
caused unintentional harm to more than one
creature in the Hundred-Acre Wood. Naturally, such
actions have made it difficult for some animals (like
Rabbit) to warm up to his ways. As a result, Rabbit has
concocted elaborate (albeit failed)
schemes "to teach Tigger a lesson" by
losing him in the woods or tricking
him into promising never to bounce
again. But Tigger is all right, really,
as Pooh, Piglet, and Christopher
Robin can attest.

EYES: Little beady eyes capable of spotting strange-looking creatures (especially in mirrors).

HEAD: Direct link between emotional disposition and degree of bounciness—e.g., when tiggers feel down, they don't bounce at all. (Bouncing requires more of an "up" feeling: see Tail.) Top of head: made of rubber. Lends itself to overall trouncy and flouncy disposition.

CHIN: Pur-posti-rus by Tigger standards.

STRIPES: Ridickerous striped pajamas provide natural camouflage defense; when hiding in trees tiggers are commonly mistaken for jagulars.

FEET: Designed for bouncing up, but not for bouncing down. (Not to be confused with jumping.)

TAIL: Spring-loaded for superb pounciness and maximum bounci-ness. Resulting bounces have unbelievable tigger-jectories. Prohibits otherwise natural ability to climb down trees. (It gets in the way.)

159

"Hey, hey, look, look— what a strange looking creature...."

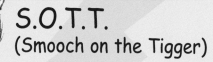

S.O.T.T.
(Smooch on the Tigger)

Behold the dawn of a new error!

I'll learn you to swing like a nightingale!

Last one there's a rotten elk!

It's the early bird that steps on the worm.

For cryin' out sakes!

Gaspedy-gasp squared!

Where the heck are my mannerisms!

Wait a minuet!

Aw, say it ain't so, buddy bear!

Heavens to Becky!

Hillarical!

Posilutely splendiforous!

Oh, contrarywise!

Stupenderous!

As I rememberize it . . .

162

Very scientifical . . .
No more time to chaise-lounge around!
Pleased as Punch 'n' Judy!
T-T-F-N! (Ta-Ta-For-Now)
T-T-F-G (Ta-Ta-For-Good)
T-T-F-E (Ta-Ta-For-Ever)

Don't be ridickerous!

TiggerTalk

Bunny Boy

Ol' Long Ears

Fluffy Tail

THE WOOD ACCORDING TO TIGGER

When Tigger calls out to "you blokes," he is, of course, speaking affectionately of his fellow Hundred-Acre Wood residents. Being absoposilutely one of a kind, he has his own special way of doing just about everything, from climbing trees to adding extra syllables to splendiferous words like "practicably" and "imaginate." Even his friends have uniquely Tiggerific nicknames:

Mrs. Kanga

Mrs. Kanga Ma'am

Donkey Boy

Piggilini

Piglet Ol' Pal

Roo Boy

Little Buddy

Pooh Boy

Buddy Bear

Beak Lips

165

FACTS & FIGURES

■ Amount anonymous buyer paid Bonhams auction house in London for Christopher Robin Milne's bear in 1996: **£4,600** ($7,084)

■ Price paid in 2000 for only known oil painting of Winnie the Pooh by E. H. Shepard by the Pavilion Gallery Museum in Assiniboine Park, Winnipeg, Canada: **£124,250** ($285,000)

■ Approximate number of annual visitors to the Donnell branch of the New York Public Library, which houses Christopher Robin's original stuffed animals: **750,000**

■ Percentage of moms of American preschoolers familiar with the character Winnie the Pooh: **98**

■ Percentage of moms of preschoolers who name Pooh as their favorite character: **60**

■ Ratio of the number of Winnie the Pooh characters sold to the number of Mickey, Minnie, and friends characters sold in 1998: **3:1**

■ Percentage of consumer usage of honey as a topping for toast or biscuits: **63**

■ Percentage of Pooh usage of honey as a topping with or without toast or biscuits: **100**

■ Number of Walt Disney Records Pooh titles that have been Gold Certified: **3**

■ Number of regular trade copies of the first edition of A. A. Milne's *Winnie-the-Pooh* printed in 1926: **35,067**

■ Minimum number of *Winnie the Pooh* books sold by 1995: **20,000,000**

■ Weight in pounds of marbelite statue commemorating Winnie the Pooh in White River, Canada: **2,000**

Acres of prairie recreation in Kane County, Illinois, named Galleons Lap: 6

CONSTRUCTION ZONE

HOUSE

167

OWL

The old beech tree in which Owl makes his home has a very long, drooping branch that bends all the way to the ground in a welcoming sort of way. Visitors may ring the bell-pull ("if an rnser is reqird") or "cnoke" on the door ("if an rnsr is not reqid"). Although Owl considers himself renowned for his brevity, his friends do not necessarily share that opinion. Virtually every occasion, circumstance, and happenstance serve as a reminder of some relevant family story, which gives Owl great pleasure to share with his company.

HEAD: Exceptional recall skills, most noticeably when retelling detailed stories about extended members of his family tree. Can spell Tuesday (sometimes) as well as his name, Wol.

EYES: Keen eyesight. Able to read (especially if no one is looking over his shoulder).

MOUTH: Remarkable diction. Has natural propensity to roll multisyllabic words off tongue.

UPPER BODY: Maintains dignified posture. Has unique ability to look wise and thoughtful even when doing nothing.

FEATHERS: Not easily ruffled. In the midst of calamitous times (such as gale force winds or floods), is able to soothe others with amusing anecdotes.

169

Owl's Cryptic Cryptograms

T he creatures of the Hundred-Acre Wood have great respect for Owl—after all, he is one of the few woodland residents who can read and spell. The wise and bookish bird has a great propensity for encyclopedic descriptions and generally knows something about something. Fortunately for Owl, however, his neighbors haven't exactly caught on to the fact that his intelligence is much better in theory than in practice.

In the puzzle below, Owl's words or phrases have been encrypted with a letter substitution code. (Example: In the cryptogram BFZZFO PJO QIIJ, B=W, F=I, Z=N, O=E, P=T, J=H, Q=P, and I=O to spell Winnie the Pooh.)

When completed, unscramble the circled letters to answer the seventh clue.

Warning: some phrases are based on Owl's wobbly spelling as seen on signs and inscriptions.

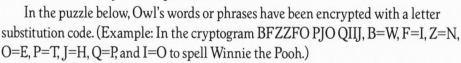

1 Visitation instructions
UWTN XMAP MG RA XANTX MN XTKMXE

_ _ _ _/_ _ _ _/_ _/_ _/_ _ _ _ _/_ _/_ _ _ _ _ _

2 Signature moniker
BY W

_ _ _

3 Knock-knock joke?
UWTH JAYVT MG RA XANX MN AYO XTKME

_ _ _ _/_ _ _ _ _/_ _/_ _/_ _ _ _/_ _/_ _ _/_ _ _ _

4 Celebratory message for a donkey
DMUI URUI LOD ZODEOD ODZODER LODZODEI

_ _ _ _/_ _ _ _/_ _ _ _ _ _ _ _/_ _ _ _ _ _ _/_ _ _ _ _ _ _

5 Irremovable honey-stuffed ursine
R LTRX BTEPTE MA PXTRO OMPDOATNN

_/_ _ _ _/_ _ _ _ _ _/_ _/_ _ _ _ _/_ _ _ _ _ _ _

6 Avian domicile
ODT BYWTXI

_ _ _/_ _ _ _ _ _

7 Why Owl deserves respect

_ _/_ _ _/_ _ _ _ _ _/_ _ _ _ _ _ _ _

(Answers on page 351)

171

By the time Wolfgang "Woolie" Reitherman directed *Winnie the Pooh and the Blustery Day*, he'd already been a veteran of The Walt Disney Studio for thirty-two years. He got his start there in 1933 at the age of twenty-three, serving as an apprentice animator on sequences in the Silly Symphony *Funny Little Bunnies* (1934); Mickey Mouse shorts, such as *Two-Gun Mickey* (1934); and the slave bit in the magic mirror in *Snow White and the Seven Dwarfs* (1937). He quickly moved up the ranks to animator, assistant supervisor, animation director, and, ultimately, producer-director. In 1963, he became the first artist in Disney history to receive full directorial recognition for the animated feature, *The Sword in the Stone*.

As director of *Winnie the Pooh and the Blustery Day* (1968) and producer

Left: Wolfgang Reitherman confers with songwriter Robert B. Sherman during a recording session.

of *Winnie the Pooh and Tigger Too* (1974), he found working on the beloved bear chronicles wasn't easy. "It was a real challenge to put Pooh on film and retain his intrinsic innocence and sweetness without making him dull or boring," Reitherman admitted in 1974. "Most cartoons nowadays rely on slapstick and a lot of action. But in *Pooh* there isn't any of that. The beauty is in the tenderness and warmth of the characters."

Reitherman overcame the difficulties by sticking to the literary origins of A. A. Milne's dialogue and E. H. Shepard's illustrations. The use of the narrator, performed by British actor Sebastian Cabot, helped the book come to life. "We show pages turning, characters springing into action from still poses, and Tigger using the printed lines like a ladder."

Reitherman continued to direct and produce all of Disney's animated features after Walt Disney's death in 1966 until his own retirement in 1980.

Right: Poster for Winnie the Pooh and Tigger Too.

Over the years, artists, directors, producers, writers, and musicians have put exceptional talent into the wonderful world of Winnie the Pooh, bringing the Silly Old Bear and his friends into the winner's circle more than two dozen times.

WINNERS

ACADEMY AWARD, Best Cartoon Short Subject (1968), Walt Disney Pictures, *Winnie the Pooh and the Blustery Day*

HUMANITAS PRIZE, Children's Animation (1989), Larry Bernard, Doug Hutchinson, Mark Zaslove, *The New Adventures of Winnie the Pooh*

EMMY AWARD, Outstanding Animated Program, Daytime (1988–1989), Karl Geurs, Mark Zaslove, *The New Adventures of Winnie the Pooh*

EMMY AWARD, Outstanding Animated Program, Daytime (1989–1990), *The New Adventures of Winnie the Pooh*

HUMANITAS PRIZE, Children's Animation (1992), Bruce Reid Schaefer, *The New Adventures of Winnie the Pooh*

GOLD CERTIFICATION (1994), Walt Disney Records, *Return to Pooh Corner*

EMMY AWARD, Outstanding Achievement in Storyboarding (1997), Phil Weinstein, *Winnie the Pooh: Boo to You Too!*

PLATINUM CERTIFICATION (1997), Walt Disney Records, *Return to Pooh Corner*

GOLD CERTIFICATION (1998), Walt Disney Records, *Take My Hand: Songs from the 100 Acre Wood*

Above: (left to right) John Lounsbery, Ollie Johnston, Milt Kahl, Larry Clemmons, Wolfgang Reitherman, Hal King, and Frank Thomas with their Oscar.

ACADEMY AWARD, Best Animated Short Film (1974), Wolfgang Reitherman, *Winnie the Pooh and Tigger Too!*

YOUNG ARTIST AWARD, Best Young Actor: Voice-Over Role (1989), Tim Hoskins, Voice of Christopher Robin, *The New Adventures of Winnie the Pooh*

EMMY AWARD, Outstanding Children's Program (1991–1992), Gaëtan Brizzi, Paul Brizzi, Ken Kessel, Jamie Mitchell, *Winnie the Pooh and Christmas Too*

GRAMMY AWARD, Best Children's Album (1995), Kenny Loggins, *Return to Pooh Corner*

GRAMMY AWARD, Best Musical Album for Children (1995), *Take My Hand: Songs From the 100 Acre Wood*

ANNIE AWARD, Best Individual Achievement: Music in a TV Production (1997), Michael and Patty Silversher, *Winnie the Pooh: Boo to You Too!*

EMMY AWARD, Outstanding Music and Lyrics (1997), Michael and Patty Silversher, *Winnie the Pooh: Boo to You Too!*

ANNIE AWARD, Outstanding Achievement in an Animated Home Video Production (1998), *Pooh's Grand Adventure: The Search for Christopher Robin*

ANNIE AWARD, Outstanding Individual Achievement for Directing in an Animated Feature (1998), Karl Geurs, *Pooh's Grand Adventure: The Search for Christopher Robin*

ANNIE AWARD, Outstanding Individual Achievement for Music in an Animated Feature (1998), Carl Johnson, *Pooh's Grand Adventure: The Search for Christopher Robin*

ANNIE AWARD, Outstanding Individual Achievement for Voice Acting by a Male Performer in an Animated Feature (1998), Paul Winchell, Voice of Tigger, *Pooh's Grand Adventure: The Search for Christopher Robin*

ANNIE AWARD, Outstanding Individual Achievement for Writing in an Animated Feature (1998), Carter Crocker, Karl Geurs, *Pooh's Grand Adventure: The Search for Christopher Robin*

EMMY AWARD, Outstanding Music Composition for a Miniseries or a Movie (1999), Carl Johnson, *Winnie the Pooh: A Valentine for You*

EMMY AWARD, Outstanding Music and Lyrics (1999), Michael and Patty Silversher, "Places in the Heart," *Winnie the Pooh: A Valentine for You*

ANNIE AWARD, Outstanding Individual Achievement for Directing in an Animated Feature (2000), Jun Falkenstein, *The Tigger Movie*

ANNIE AWARD, Outstanding Individual Achievement for Music in an Animated Feature (2000), Richard M. and Robert B. Sherman, "Round My Family Tree," *The Tigger Movie*

Right: Director Wolfgang Reitherman with his award for Winnie the Pooh and the Blustery Day.

ANNIE AWARD, Outstanding Individual Achievement for Voice Acting by a Male Performer in an Animated Feature (2000), Nikita Hopkins, Voice of Roo, *The Tigger Movie*

SIERRA AWARD, Best Family Film (2000), *The Tigger Movie*

GRAMMY AWARD, Best Children's Album (2001), Kenny Loggins, *More Songs from Pooh Corner*

A Field Guide to
Fierce Animals

Members of the woozle and heffalump family (*Mellis ereptor*) vary considerably in color, size, and shape. They tend to be nocturnal and ferocious, often appearing in dreams and nightmares. Rather than hunting for their food in the wild, they prefer to steal larder from other unsuspecting honey consumers.

NOTE: Most seasoned *Mellis ereptor* watchers will not have difficulty recognizing a heffalump or woozle; however, even experts commonly mistake species. These cunning creatures adapt remarkably to their environments and skillfully imitate other species.

JACK-IN-THE-BOX WOOZLE
(*Wuztela saltanda*)
DESCRIPTION: boxy body, often with letters that spell "hunny" and spring coil neck that can compress within body or pop outside it; head varies in color, but is usually blue, red, or green; ball-like nose. VOICE: high-pitched squeals and guffaws. FOOD: honey. HABITS: likes to let tongue hang out while laughing.

SPOTTED WOOZLE
(*Wuztela maculosa*)
DESCRIPTION: weasel-like body, red spots; ball-like nose. VOICE: varied shrieks and singsong cries. FOOD: honey. HABITS: likes to balance on tail.

HORN-NOSED WOOZLE
(*Wuztela cornus vultus*)
DESCRIPTION: weasel-like body,
with long trumpetlike proboscis;
walks upright. VOICE: trumpet-
ing toots. FOOD: honey. HABITS:
prefers to march.

STRIPED WOOZLE
(*Wuztela funium*)
DESCRIPTION: somewhat larger than the Spotted Woozle, it has horizontal light and dark purple stripes across entire body; small black nose; wry smile.
VOICE: confusil sounds. FOOD: honey.
HABITS: prefers sidling up to honeypots.

CHECKERED HEFFALUMP
(*Helefus quadratus*)
DESCRIPTION: entire elephantlike body is covered in checks; head can expand to larger size than body; body can expand until heffalump reaches gargantuan proportions.
VOICE: varying trumpets.
FOOD: honey.
HABITS: likes to toss Pooh Bears with trunk.

HOT-AIR HEFFALUMP
(*Helefus aeris fervens*)
DESCRIPTION: usually red, green, or blue; head, eyes, and nose make up entire body, which is shaped like a hot-air balloon; trunk has powerful honey-sucking power; honeypots often attach to end of proboscis.
VOICE: baritone blasts. FOOD: honey.
HABITS: can unexpectedly pop.

BEE-BACKED HEFFALUMP
(*Helefus apis tergo*)
DESCRIPTION: elephantlike head with antennae; bumblebeelike body with wings attached at back of neck.
VOICE: buzzing trumpets. FOOD: honey. HABITS: can fly as need arises.

BATHING HEFFALUMP
(*Helefus natans*)
DESCRIPTION: always seen in striped bathing suit; likes to wear hats; is fat.
VOICE: slurping noises. *FOOD*: honey and lollipops. *HABITS*: often leads other heffalumps in grand marches.

SKIP-ROPE HEFFALUMP
(*Helefus tripudii*)
DESCRIPTION: females tend to be green and pink; males, blue and white; also seen in striped and polka-dot varieties.
VOICE: childlike giggles and laughter.
FOOD: honey. *HABITS*: can morph into squares and balls, and twist themselves up in knots.

Next to Mickey Mouse, Winnie the Pooh is the most sought-after character in all of Disney's Magic Kingdoms. Whether it's taking a romp through the Hundred-Acre Wood, sharing a meal, finding a delightful collectible, or simply enjoying the ultimate bear hug, there's more than one way to spend time with the delightful Pooh Bear.

■ Pooh's Hunny Hunt attraction at Tokyo Disneyland is a grand tour through the Hundred-Acre Wood featuring Pooh and all his friends. Travel through this trackless dark ride in self-propelled honeypots and join Pooh in his exciting adventures and wild dreams as he sets out in search of his favorite food.

■ Have a "Thotful" moment and an ideal photo op with Winnie the Pooh and his pals as they can often be found in a quiet little corner in Critter Country, Disneyland Park.

■ Hold on to your honeypots as you travel through the giant storybook pages of The Many Adventures of Winnie the Pooh at Walt Disney World. Get whisked through a blustery

ATTRACTIONS

&

ADVENTURES

day in the Hundred-Acre Wood as Owl's house topples, Piglet is swept away by the storm, Tigger bounces into an active game of hide-and-seek, and honey-stealing heffalumps and woozles abound.

■ Indulge in memorabilia madness at specialty shops dedicated to the denizens of the Hundred-Acre Wood: Pooh Corner in Critter Country at Disneyland; Downtown Disney at Walt Disney World; Fantasyland at Tokyo Disneyland; The Briar Patch shop in Frontierland and Pooh's Thotful Spot in Fantasyland at Walt Disney World.

■ Dine with your Hundred-Acre pals at special Walt Disney World locales. Look for the giant Pooh, Tigger, Eeyore, and Piglet topiaries outside the Crystal Palace on Main Street, which offers an all-you-can-eat buffet with Pooh and friends. Pooh has also been known to dine with guests at Olivia's café in Disney's Old Key West Resort at a special Winnie the Pooh-themed character breakfast, and during the dinner hour at the 1900 Park Fare Restaurant at Disney's Grand Floridian Resort.

■ Watch the adventurous antics that take place in the Hundred-Acre Wood in the 25-minute stage show *Winnie the Pooh and Friends Too* at Le Théâtre du Château in Fantasyland at Disneyland Paris. Stick around before or after performances to meet Winnie the Pooh, Tigger, and Eeyore in person.

Piglet's Honey Cake

The next time you're celebrating a happy event, a holiday, or a guest of honor, sweeten the occasion with a slice of honey cake. Whether served unadorned or fancified with frosting, this recipe is sure to win over the hearts— and taste buds—of all the honey lovers in your neck of the woods.

INGREDIENTS:

3 large eggs
1 cup sugar
1 cup honey
1/2 cup cool strong brewed coffee
1 cup vegetable oil
2 1/2 cups sifted all-purpose flour
2 teaspoons baking powder
1/2 teaspoon baking soda
1/4 teaspoon salt
1 teaspoon cinnamon
1/2 teaspoon ground cloves
1/2 teaspoon allspice
1/4 teaspoon ginger
1/2 cup chopped hazelnuts or walnuts
zest of 1/2 orange
1 tablespoon cognac

1. Preheat oven to 350° F. Grease Bundt pan or square 9" x 9" pan.
2. Lightly beat the eggs. Add sugar gradually and whisk until mixture is light and fluffy.
3. Blend the honey and coffee together and stir into oil. Stir into egg mixture.
4. Sift together flour, baking powder, baking soda, salt, cinnamon, ground cloves, allspice, and ginger. Make a well in center of flour and add egg mixture, whisking until combined well.
5. Stir in chopped nuts, orange zest, and cognac.
6. Pour batter into pan and bake in center of oven 45–55 minutes, or until tester comes out clean. Cool on wire rack.

Piglet's variation: To sate that extra sweet tooth, dust with confectioners' sugar or spread with a fudgy frosting.

Serves 8 to 10

191

Piglet's BIG Movie

Piglet's BIG Movie brings "the little pink guy" to center stage as the inhabitants of the Hundred-Acre Wood learn that you're never too small to do great things. After Piglet puts the finishing touches on his special scrapbook, he's eager to join his friends who are on their way to a honey harvest, but they say he's too small. Feeling inadequate, Piglet wanders off on his own. When the honey harvest goes awry, Pooh and the others seek shelter at Piglet's house where they find the scrapbook—

but no Piglet!—and so a new quest commences. As Pooh and the others use the scrapbook's drawings as a guide to help them find him, they're touched by the love evident in the illustrations Piglet has made of his friends' many exploits, and realize that Piglet has been a very important part of their adventures in a way they never recognized before. And they appreciate more fully the heroic act he performs to save *them* when they're trying to save *him*! With new songs by Carly Simon, *Piglet's BIG Movie* is a spirited, warmhearted, and worthy addition to the Pooh panoply of films.

How to Be B-b-b-brave

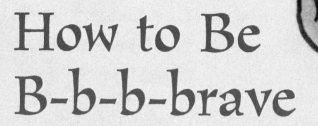

It's hard to be brave when you're a very small animal, but even small animals can be brave sometimes. Those lacking in pluck might find comfort in following Piglet's examples:

■ Look fear right in the face and conquer it (only if it doesn't conquer you first).

■ Avoid trouble. Stay away from places that are not suitable for small and frightfully fearful animals.

■ If you can't hear it, it can't hurt you. Keep a pillowcase handy for putting over your head and covering your ears.

■ If you can't see it, it can't hurt you. (See above.)

■ Hum (in a "what-shall-we-do-now?" kind of way).

■ Try not to think about heffalumps and whether or not they're fond of Piglets.

■ Don't look down (in the event the ground is far below)!

■ Don't look up (in the event a jagular is lurking in the treetops)!

■ Tremble on the inside.

■ Remember that smallness can be a very useful quality in expeditions, adventures, and rescues.

■ When the waters are swirling around you in a great big whirlpool, just remember that a rescue is being thought of.

Reel-to-Reel Pooh

When Walt Disney first adapted A. A. Milne's stories about the Hundred-Acre Wood for the silver screen in *Winnie the Pooh and the Honey Tree* (1966), the film was so well received by American audiences that it warranted the release of two theatrical sequels, one of which won an Academy Award. Since then, Pooh and his friends have had many new adventures in educational films, an Emmy Award–winning television series, and videos that continue to win new generations of fans:

FILMS

Winnie the Pooh and the Honey Tree (1966)
Winnie the Pooh and the Blustery Day (1968)
Winnie the Pooh and Tigger Too (1974)
The Many Adventures of Winnie the Pooh (1977)
Winnie the Pooh and a Day for Eeyore (1983)
The Tigger Movie (2000)

TELEVISION SERIES

Welcome to Pooh Corner (1983–1995)
*The New Adventures of Winnie
    the Pooh* (1988–1993; 1995–1996)
The Book of Pooh (2001–)

EDUCATIONAL FILMS

Winnie the Pooh Discovers the Seasons (1981)
Winnie the Pooh's ABC of Me (1990)

VIDEOS

Winnie the Pooh and Christmas Too (1991)
Winnie the Pooh: Boo To You Too! (1996)
Winnie the Pooh Learning: Growing Up (1996)
Winnie the Pooh Learning: Helping Others (1997)
*Pooh's Grand Adventure: The Search for
    Christopher Robin* (1997)
Winnie the Pooh Playtime: Cowboy Pooh (1997)
Winnie the Pooh Playtime: Detective Tigger (1997)
The Making of Winnie the Pooh (1998)
Winnie the Pooh Playtime: Fun 'N' Games (1998)
Winnie the Pooh Playtime: Happy Pooh Day (1998)
Winnie the Pooh Learning: Making Friends (1998)
Winnie the Pooh Learning: Sharing & Caring (1998)
Winnie the Pooh: A Valentine for You (1998)
Winnie the Pooh: Frankenpooh (1999)
Winnie the Pooh Learning: Working Together (1999)
Winnie the Pooh Playtime: Pooh Party (1999)
Winnie the Pooh: Seasons of Giving (1999)
Winnie the Pooh: Spookable Pooh (1999)
Winnie the Pooh: Un-Valentine's Day (1999)
The Book of Pooh: Stories from the Heart (2001)

197

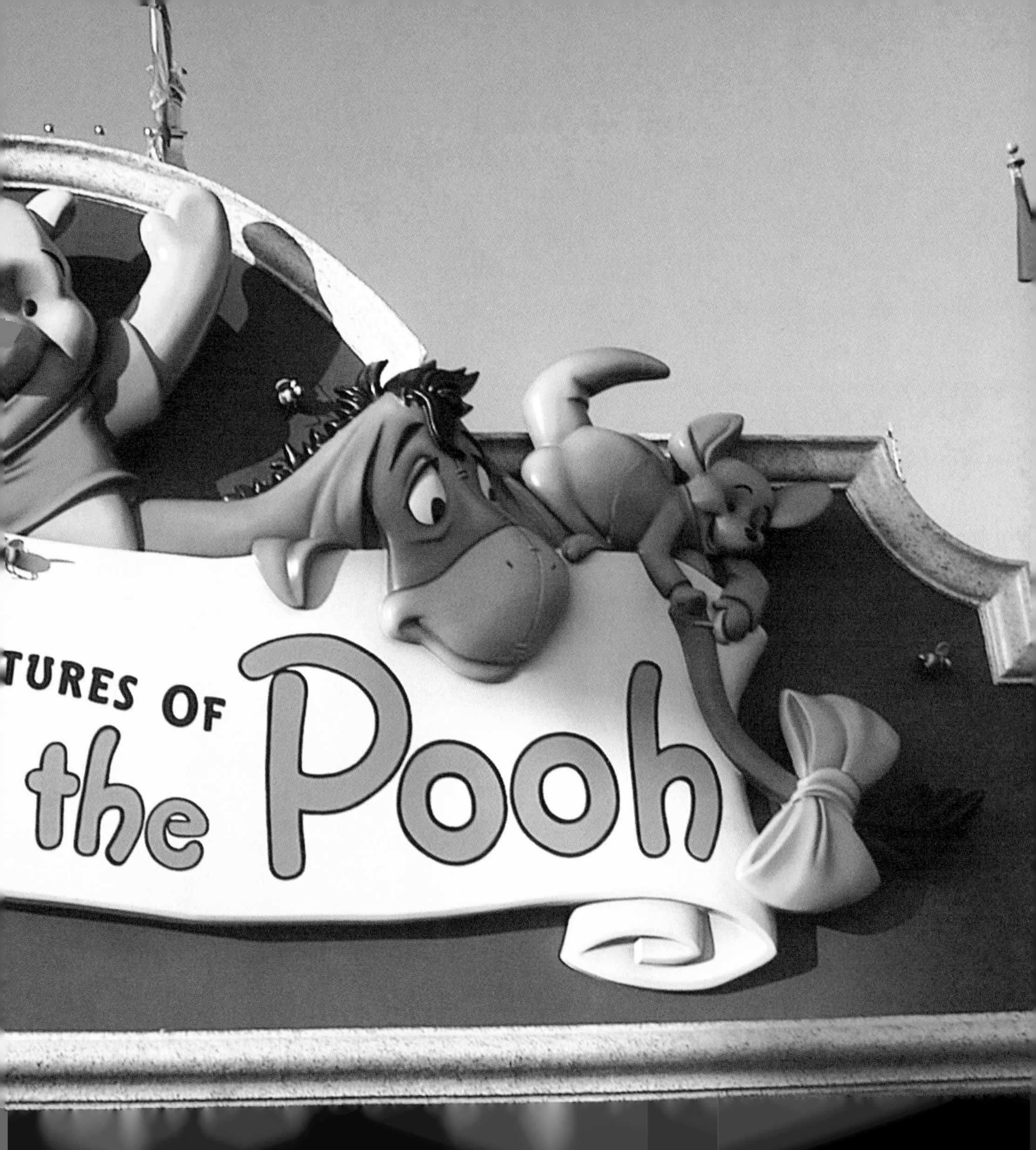
TURES OF
the Pooh

Owl's Family Bedtime Stories

(or How to Cure Insomnia)

When it comes to amusing anecdotes, nobody quite tells a tale the way Owl does. A master of long words like "encyclopedia" and "rhododendron," Owl has served to distract listeners in times of unfortunate predicaments, turbulent weather, or sudden and temporary immersions into rivers. Owl's nostalgic renditions have a way of boring deep into the hearts of his audience and, putting them in the most tranquil states of mind.

Have you heard the one about...

AN AUNT, unnerved by the constant practicing of Aunt Clara the screech owl, who once laid a seagull's egg by mistake...?

UNCLE CLYDE, a very independent barn owl who didn't give a hoot for tradition, who became enamored of a pussycat and went to sea in a beautiful pea-green boat...?

AUNT CLARA, who during the mild zephyr of '67 (or was it '76), went to visit her cousin, a screech owl who was gifted on the glockenspiel and who also sang soprano in the Royal Opera...?

AUNT OPHELIA, who, upon joining the Royal Opera, sang with a voice that squeaked like clean dishes...?

GREAT UNCLE ROBERT, who had reached the ripe old age of 103 (though he wouldn't admit to being older than 97), and the family felt a celebration was in order...?

A DISTANT COUSIN, who became so frightened during a flood that he turned prematurely gray, and was often mistaken for an arctic snow owl...?

GREAT UNCLE TORBIT, the dashing good cook, who once made a three-minute egg in a mere 45 seconds...?

UNCLE HORATIO, who used to dive straight down in flight? He went on to take third place in a flying contest in Rome, after which he went to Acapulco (or was it Topeka?)...?

201

"I do some of my best thinking— when I'm asleep."

STILL LIFE *with* BEAR

To date, five statues in Canada and England celebrate the legacy of Winnie the Pooh and the little black bear that helped start it all.

1. **Assiniboine Park Zoo, Winnipeg, Manitoba, Canada** On permanent display among Canada's second largest animal collection is an American black bear commemorated in bronze. The 25-foot statue is of Lieutenant Harry Colebourn and his bear cub Winnie (short for Winnipeg), which he purchased from a trapper. Read the story of the original Winnie on the statue's plaque erected on the front grounds of the zoo's Kinsmen Discovery Centre.

2. **London Zoo, Regent's Park, London, England** In 1981, the Zoological Society of London erected the first statue in honor of the literary Winnie the Pooh and his creators. Sculptor Lorne McKean created the life-size bronze statue of Winnipeg, the beloved female black bear that lived at the zoo from 1914 to 1934. Part of the inscription reads: "She gave her name to Winnie the Pooh, and A. A. Milne and Ernest Shepard gave Winnie the Pooh to the rest of the world."

3. **White River Township, Ontario, Canada** In memory of the officer who purchased Winnie, artist Orville Mowers carved a nine-foot rendition of Lieutenant Colebourn and the cub. The wooden sculpture was unveiled at the White River Tourist Information Centre in 1989.

4. **White River Township, Ontario, Canada** In 1992, the community of White River, celebrated as the birthplace of Winnipeg the bear, erected a commemorative statue in the heart of town, designed by Disney Studio artists Anthony Van Bruggen and Alvaro Cervantes. The 2,000-pound marbelite Winnie the Pooh sitting in a tree with his treasured honeypot was built by Canadian sculptor George Barone.

5. **London Zoo, Regent's Park, London, England** In 1995, the citizens of Manitoba, Canada, bequeathed to the London Zoo a statue of Lieutenant Colebourn and Winnipeg. Colebourn's old military unit, the 34th Fort Garry Horse Regiment, unveiled the statue by the Children's Zoo. The bronze statue was created by sculptor Bill Epp to commemorate the bear's Canadian heritage.

Tips for Trackers

While the majority of Pooh's exploratory enterprises are in the pursuit of honey, there are occasions when the mystery of an unidentified imprint in the snow may sound the call to adventure. When hunting in the woods, it's important to have a watchful eye, a story or two to pass the time, and a few rules to follow, for as Pooh has often said, "You can never tell with paw marks."

1 Once you discover prints, you may start tracking.

2 Invite a friend to join you, in the event the tracks have been made by hostile animals.

3 It is often necessary to catch up with whatever it is you're tracking before determining exactly what it is you're tracking.

4 When someone stops and points excitedly, you may jump up yourself. Jump up and down once or twice again in "an exercising sort of way" to show you were not frightened.

5 It is a fearful event to discover that whatever it is that made the tracks has been joined by something else.

6 Sometimes it is.

7 Sometimes it isn't.

8 Before hostile animals are spotted, you may remember something you forgot to do yesterday and cannot do tomorrow. This is an acceptable reason to leave and be out of all danger.

Winnie the Pooh

and Tigger Too

O N ONE PARTICULARLY SUNNY MORNING, Winnie the Pooh, who was a bear of very little brain, was trying very hard to think of something. "Think, think, think, think, think … think, think." Pooh thought, tapping his head.

And while he was thinking, all of a sudden—*OOF!* He found himself flat on his back, face-to-face with the bounciest creature in the Hundred-Acre Wood.

"Hello Pooh! G-rrrrr … I'm Tigger! T-I-double-Guh-Rrr! That spells Tigger!" said Tigger.

"Ha, ha, I know," laughed Pooh. "You've bounced me before."

"I did?" asked Tigger. He pressed his nose close to Pooh's for a better look. "Oh yeah! I recognize you . . . You're the one that's stuffed with fluff!" Then he pulled Pooh up and shook his hand. "Well, I gotta go now. I gotta lotta bouncin' to do. Ha-ha-ha-hooo . . . T-T-F-N! Ta-Ta-For-Now!"

Meanwhile, in another corner of the Hundred-Acre Wood, Piglet was busy sweeping the leaves from his doorstep when—*OOF!* He received a loud and violent bounce.

"Grrrrr, oh hello, Piglet. I'm Tigger!" said Tigger to his pinned-down pal.

"Oh Tigger, you sca-ca-ca-cared me," Piglet stammered.

"Aw, shucks," said Tigger, flattered by Piglet's compliment. "That was just one of my little bounces. I'm savin' my best bounce for Old Long Ears," Tigger explained. "Ta-ta!" And off he bounced, yet again, this time headed directly for Rabbit's house.

Rabbit was humming merrily in his wonderful garden, picking the last of his ripe, juicy carrots. Tigger crashed into Rabbit and sent his carrots flying everywhere. "Hello Rabbit! I'm Tigger! T-I-double-Guh—"

"Oh please . . . please, don't spell it!" Rabbit sputtered angrily. "Tigger! Oh why don't you ever stop bouncing?"

"Why, that's what Tiggers do best! Oo . . . hoo, hoo, hooo!" And with a song and dance, Tigger cheerfully bounced away, leaving Rabbit to stew in his garden.

Later that day, Rabbit decided to call an important meeting to do something about Tigger's bounciness. Rabbit explained all the details of his very clever plan.

"I've got a splendid idea. Now listen . . . we'll take Tigger for a long explore, see . . . someplace where he's never been!" Rabbit said with a sly laugh. "And we'll lose him there."

Pooh, who had fallen asleep, woke up with a startling snort. "Lose him?" he asked.

"Oh we'll find him again next morning," Rabbit promised enthusiastically. "And, mark my words,

he'll be a humble Tigger, a small and sad Tigger ... an 'Oh Rabbit, am I glad to see you' Tigger ... and it'll take the bounces out of him, that's why!"

So, it was agreed that Rabbit, Pooh, Piglet, and Tigger would start the next morning, which incidentally turned out cold and misty. As Tigger kept bouncing farther and farther into the mist, Rabbit thought it was a good time to lose Tigger. "Now's our chance! Quick ... in here ... hide!" he said diving into a nearby hollowed log.

Rabbit poked his head out of the log to see if the coast was clear. When there was no sight of Tigger, he chuckled at his own brilliant, successful plan. But then a familiar sound made Rabbit's ears perk up: "Halloooooooooo ..."

"Halloooo!" came Tigger's booming voice. "Hey, you blokes, where are you?" he shouted. But no one answered, so he bounced off into the misty woods with a fading "Hallooooo ..."

Rabbit peeked out of the log again as soon as he thought it was safe. "Hooray ... hooray ... we've done it!" he shouted when he saw no sign of Tigger.

214

Right: Pooh falls asleep while Rabbit plans. Storyboard art.

"Now, come on," he urged, helping Piglet and Pooh out of the log. "Hurry! Let's head for home."

Well, Rabbit was certain everything was going according to plan. And so it seemed to be. But sometime later, Rabbit stood at the edge of the very same sandpit he thought he saw ten minutes earlier. And ten minutes before that. "Hmm, it's a funny thing how everything looks the same in the mist," he told the others.

Now, Pooh was getting tired of seeing the same sandpit. "Uh, er, say, Rabbit, how would it be if as soon as we're out of sight of this old pit, we just try to find it again?" asked Pooh.

Baffled, Rabbit asked, "What's the good of that?"

"Well, y' see," Pooh suggested, "we keep looking for home, but we keep finding this pit. So I just thought that if we looked for this pit, we might find home."

"I don't see much sense in that," Rabbit said curtly. "If I walked away from this pit and then walked back to it . . . of course I should find it. I'll prove it to

Left: "Hide!" Storyboard art. Above: Tigger comes very close, and Pooh is ordered to "shush!" Storyboard art.

"It's a funny thing

how everything

looks the same

in a mist."

you—wait here!" And so, Rabbit marched off into the mist.

So Pooh and Piglet waited in the mist for Rabbit. And they waited . . . and waited . . . and waited . . . .

"Wha . . . wha . . . what was that, Pooh?" Piglet said, when a loud noise rumbled in the pit by Piglet's ear.

"My tummy rumbled." Pooh giggled. "Now, then, come on—let's go home. There are twelve pots of honey in my cupboard an' they have been calling to my tummy."

"They have?" asked Piglet, who was very impressed.

"Yes, Piglet," said Pooh as he helped his struggling friend out of the sandpit. "I couldn't hear them before because Rabbit would talk. I think I know where they're calling from, so come on—we'll just follow my tummy."

Well, they walked off together, and for a long time Piglet said nothing, so as not to interrupt Pooh's honeypots. And, sure enough, as the mist got thinner, and just as

Preceding pages: Pooh and Piglet in the mist. Production still.

Piglet was beginning to know where he was—*OOF! OOF!* Tigger bounced out of nowhere and pinned Pooh and Piglet to the ground.

"Hey...hey...hello there, you two blokes! Say, where is Old Long Ears?" asked Tigger, stretching his ears like Rabbit's.

"He must still be missing in the mist," said Pooh.

"Well, leave it to me," said a very confident Tigger. "I'll bounce him out of there. T-T-F-N...Ta-Ta-For-Now! Hoo, hoo, hoo, hooooo!"

Meanwhile, Rabbit was still wandering around in the mist. By now he was lost and bewildered, and to make matters worse, his mind was beginning to play tricks on him. Every little sound made him jump, and every little jump made another sound. All the croaking frogs and chomping caterpillars worked poor Rabbit into such a fright that he bolted out of the misty woods as fast as he could, when *BOING!*—Rabbit found himself nose to nose with Tigger.

"Hello, Rabbit!" greeted Tigger.

"Tigger!" gasped Rabbit. "B-bu-bu...but...you're supposed to be lost."

"Tiggers never get lost, Bunny Boy!" Tigger said, patting Rabbit's cheeks.

Left: Rabbit is lost and frantic. Cel setup.

"Never get lost?" Rabbit whined.

"Of course not!" Tigger proclaimed, helping Rabbit up. "Come on Rabbit, let's go home...hang on!" And as Rabbit held tightly onto Tigger's tail, Tigger yanked him along as he bounced and hoo-hoo-hoo-hooooed all they way home. So Rabbit was now a humiliated Rabbit. A lost-and-found rabbit. An oh-why-oh-why-do-these-things-happen-to-me Rabbit.

The next day, the first snowfall had covered the Hundred-Acre Wood. On this fine day, Roo was waiting for Tigger to take him out to play.

"Mama? When is Tigger gonna get here?" he asked, bouncing on top of the mailbox.

"Be patient, dear," said Kanga as she swept the snow away. "He'll be—" Before Kanga could finish, Tigger came bouncing through the newly fallen snow, dousing Roo with a spray of white powder that knocked him off the mailbox. "Wheee! Well, here I am," announced Tigger. "Roo, are you ready for some bouncin'?"

"Yeah...you and me are good bouncers," said Roo, eager to go. So, Tigger and Roo bounced happily away alongside the snowbanks, and Kanga, looking after them, reminded Tigger to have Roo home in time for his nap.

Roo and Tigger hadn't bounced too far into the woods before they came across a frozen pond, where they spotted Rabbit humming blissfully and skating perfect figure eights.

"Can Tiggers ice-skate as fancy as Mr. Rabbit?" asked Roo admiringly.

"Can Tiggers ice-skate! Why, that's what Tiggers do best!" bragged Tigger. He jumped out onto the ice to demonstrate. Tigger skated gracefully on one foot, then the other. But when he tried to skate on his springy tail, he slipped on the ice, spun out of control, and crashed right into Rabbit. 'Round and 'round they spun until they slid off the ice and skidded headfirst into a snow-bank just outside Rabbit's front door.

"Oh, why does it always have to be me?" cried Rabbit. "Why, oh why, oh why?"

Tigger popped out of the snow. "Yecch!" he said, spitting out a mouthful of snow. "Tiggers don't like ice-skating!"

So Tigger and Roo went farther into the Hundred-Acre Wood, looking for something that Tiggers do best.

Right: "Let's bounce!" Storyboard art.

223

Roo looked up at the towering branches over their heads. "I bet you could climb trees, huh, Tigger?" he said.

"Climb trees!" chortled Tigger. "That's what Tiggers do best! Only Tiggers don't climb trees...they bounce 'em! Come on, let's go!"

So Roo hopped up onto Tigger's shoulders, and Tigger bounced from branch to branch to branch until he reached the very top of the tree. "Hoo, hoo, hoo, hoo! Some bouncin', huh?" he laughed. But he took one look down and locked his arms and legs around the tree. "Say," he said with his eyes glued shut, "how did this tree get so high?"

Suddenly, the treetop start to swing back and forth. "Hey, what's happening now?" yowled Tigger. He opened a brave eye and looked down to see Roo swinging gleefully from Tigger's tail. "S-s-s-ss-s-stop that kid, please..." begged Tigger. "S-T-O-P. Stop! You're rockin' the forest!"

While Tigger was stuck up in the treetop, Pooh and Piglet were busy tracking some footprints around a bush. Mysteriously, the footprints kept on multiplying as they followed them. Pooh and Piglet were feeling a little anxious now, in case the company of animals in front of them was of hostile intent. Then they heard a very loud noise.

Right: "How did this tree get so high?" Storyboard art.

"Hal-looooo!" it said.

"Hey, Tigger, it's Pooh and Piglet!" Roo shouted up to Tigger. Then shouting below, he cried: "Pooh! Piglet!"

"Why," Pooh said to Piglet, "it's only Tigger and Roo...come on!" They ran to the base of the tree and waved up to their friends. "Hello, Roo, what are you and Tigger doing up there?" asked Pooh.

"I'm all right," Roo giggled, "but Tigger's stuck."

And, sure enough, there was Tigger, still dangling from the highest tree branch, holding on for his dear life, wailing: "Help, somebody...please...get Christopher Robin!"

Well, it wasn't long before word got back to Christopher Robin and the others that Tigger was in trouble. Soon Christopher Robin, Rabbit, Kanga, Piglet, and Pooh were all standing at the base of the tree, looking up at Tigger.

"That's good!" Rabbit exclaimed "Tigger can't bounce anybody up there."

Preceding pages: "A whole new set of tracks!"
Storyboard art. Above: Piglet and Pooh run to see
Tigger and Roo. Cel setup.

"Come on, everyone," Christopher Robin said as he took off his coat to use as a net. "Let's hold a corner of my coat. You're first, Roo...jump!"

"Try not to fall too fast, dear," Kanga warned as Roo jumped out of the tree with a loud *whee-E-E-E-e-e!*

"You're next, Tigger—jump!" Christopher Robin added.

"Jump?" Tigger cried, still clinging to the tree. "Tiggers don't jump... they bounce!"

"Then bounce down!" suggested Pooh.

"Ah...don't be ridickerous...Tiggers only bounce up!" said Tigger.

Christopher Robin said, "You can climb down, Tigger!"

But he didn't budge. "Tiggers can't climb down," he protested, hemming and hawing. "Ah...ah...because...ah...ah...ah...their tails get in the way!"

Tigger's words were music to Rabbit's ears. "Hooray! That settles it!" he

shouted, happily. "If he won't jump...and he can't climb down...then we'll just have to leave him up there forever!"

"Forever?" Tigger worried. He couldn't bear the thought. "Oh, if I ever get outta dis...I promise never to bounce again—never!" said Tigger solemnly.

Meanwhile, Rabbit was crazed with delight. "I heard that, Tigger," he cried. "He promised! Did you hear him promise?" shouted Rabbit.

Finally, Christopher Robin said, "You can let go now, Tigger!"

And ever so slowly and ever so carefully, Tigger managed to work his way down to good old terra firma.

"I'm so happy, I feel like bouncin'," he said, kissing the ground.

Rabbit was quick to scold him. "Ah . . . ah . . . You promised! You promised!"

Tigger's happiness slowly drained out of his face, "Oh . . . oh, I did, didn't I? Ya mean . . . I can't ever bounce? Again?"

"Never!" shouted Rabbit, pounding his hand into his fist.

Tigger's shoulders drooped, and his tail sagged. "Never?" Tigger's lip quivered. "Not even just one teensy-weensy bounce?"

"Not even a smidgen of a bounce." Rabbit said defiantly.

230

Above: A frightened Tigger becomes a dejected Tigger. Storyboard art.

"Oh the poor dear. That's too bad," said Kanga, sorry to see Tigger slumping away into the woods.

Roo was sad, too. "Christopher Robin," he said, tugging at his shirt, "I like the old bouncy Tigger best!"

"So do I, Roo," agreed Christopher Robin.

"I do, too!" Piglet chimed in.

"Me, too!" said Roo again.

"Of course, we all do," said Kanga in her most motherly voice, "Don't you agree, Rabbit?"

"Oh … all right," said Rabbit, giving in. "I guess I like the old Tigger better, too."

Suddenly, *BOING!* Before Rabbit knew what was happening, Tigger bounced him. "Oh boy … ha … ya mean, I can have my bounce back …?" Tigger asked eagerly. "Come on, Rabbit!" he cheered, pulling him off the ground. "Let's you and me bounce, huh?"

"Good heavens!" Rabbit scoffed. "Me bounce?"

"Why certainly!" said Tigger, holding up one of Rabbit's big feet. "Look ... you got the feet for it!"

"I have?" asked Rabbit, doubtfully.

"Sure. Come on, try it!" Tigger started dancing around Rabbit to show him how easy it was to bounce. "It makes you feel just ... g-g-g-g-great!"

Rabbit decided to give it a try. First he tried a little one, then a bigger one, then an even bigger one. In no time, Rabbit had a huge smile plastered on his face and was bouncing happily alongside Tigger. So everyone joined in the fun, and Christopher Robin, Kanga, Roo, Piglet, and Pooh all bounced their way through another joyful day in the Hundred-Acre Wood. ■

What Tiggers Do Best!

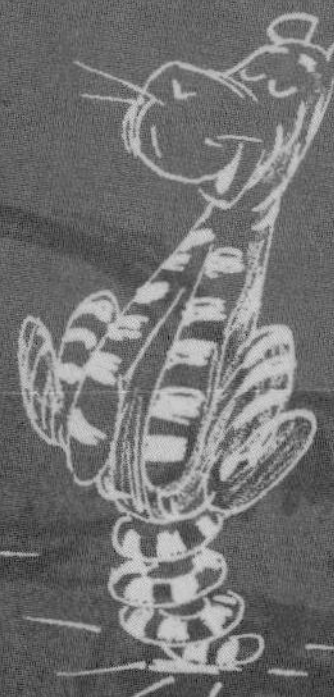

One of the most wonderful things about
tiggers is that they like to have fun, fun,
fun, fun, fun—after all, it's one of the many
things tiggers do best. And being exceptional creatures, tiggers do *many* things best, although other
animals in the Hundred-Acre Wood might disagree.
Some of these talents may result in breaking things
up, knocking things down, and leaving the place a
mess, but they're still what tiggers do best:

Ice-skate   ~~Fly~~   ~~Ski~~

~~Swim~~   Climb trees

~~Never get lost~~   ~~Garden~~

~~Eat haycorns~~   ~~Eat thistles~~

Play ~~Pooh~~ Sticks

~~Accept challenges~~

~~Play tricks~~   ~~Pop corn~~

~~Stay up all night~~   ~~Eat honey~~

~~Weed carrots~~   Everything

Bounce!

235

W-D-Double-L-A-O-B

In times of great distress, including major property damage, natural disasters of mountainous proportion, or simply being stuck out on a limb, the best plan of action is often the bounciest. Such a plan calls for the kind of bounce that only the very bestest bouncers can bounce—the W-D-Double-L-A-O-B (aka the Whoop-de-Dooper Loop-de-Looper Alley-Ooper Bounce). *Remember: half this bounce is ninety percent mental!*

To trigger the W-D-Double-L-A-O-B, follow these five simple steps:

STEP 1.
Swing your legs up high.

STEP 2.
Twist your tail in tight.

STEP 3.
Wind up all your springs.

236

STEP 4.
Keep your eyes
fixated straight ahead.

STEP 5.
Let it all loose!

SAFETY RULES
& REGULARATIONS

Rule #1:
Always bounce in
a well-lit area.

Rule #the next one:
Never bounce near
an open flame.

Rule #3:
Never bounce
after eating.

Rule #4:
Do not forget Rule #3.

237

RABBIT

One of the busiest animals in the Hundred-Acre Wood, Rabbit is usually telling others what to do, making official plans, or tending to agricultural matters. Being of a very practical disposition, Rabbit generally prefers to do useful things rather than playing or going on adventures. Instead of waiting for things to come to him, he will go out to fetch them, marking the sign of a true leader.

EYES: Never loses sight of what's really important—very likely due to diet rich in vitamin A.

EARS: Have tendency to twist, wring, or otherwise entwine during situations of extreme angst. Also source of inspiration for nickname, "Ole Long Ears."

HEAD: Has brain (like Owl and Eeyore), unlike other animals in the Hundred-Acre Wood who have fluff. Is leaderly, thinking, and forward.

MOUTH: Occasionally attempts to sound like Nobody or Somebody other than Rabbit when hungry Pooh Bears come calling.

HAND: Has exceptionally green thumb. Gardening skills outrival those of all other creatures in the forest.

FARMER RABBIT'S ALMANAC

Rabbit's Gardening Tips & Philosophy

The secret to great gardening is knowing when to plant!

Keeping a scarecrow in the garden can be a good thing, unless you have many very small and frightfully fearful friends.

When in doubt, do your gardening by the book. *The Bunny's Farm Companion* should be required reading for all tillers of the soil.

Seeds cannot grow in soil that's rough and dry.

Mark your calendar! The first day of fall following the last day of summer is harvest day.

Best to choose seeds that will have the extremely good sense to sprout after you plant them in your garden.

If you find a hungry bug in your prize tomato patch, don't feed it any tomatoes—no matter how cute it may be. It will only tell its friends, and your tomatoes will be history.

In order to weed properly, you must be able to distinguish a weed from a carrot top.

Rabbit's Tried-and-True Favorite Crops

carrots
pumpkins
rutabagas
tomatoes
cabbage
corn

Gardening 101

The most important thing to a Rabbit is his garden, but not just anyone can be a gardener. Growing and maintaining a garden is a great deal of very hard work. However, with a little bit of dedication and a lot of love, even the novice may turn up a green thumb. Your basic needs for a proper garden include:

seeds
patch of ground
lots of moisture
dark, rich earth
plenty of sunshine
watering can
shovel
rake or hoe
hat
wheelbarrow (for all those carrots!)

Reader's Secrets

• Plants have a lot to say if you take the time to listen.
• My seeds sprout faster when I sing lullabies to them.

The 5-Step Carrot

1. Poke a hole in the soil
2. Drop in seed
3. Cover
4. Water
5. Admire, then harvest!

Rabbit's Honeyed Carrots

The next time you invite a bear for lunch (or the next time a bear invites himself for lunch), and you don't want your entire jar of honey to disappear, try serving this favorite family recipe. You don't need a whole jar of honey, and chances are good that even after extra servings of carrots, your bear won't get stuck in the door.

1 1/2 lbs. pounds peeled and sliced carrots
2 tablespoons butter
1/4 cup honey
2 tablespoons chopped parsley
1 tablespoon fresh lemon juice

1. Place carrots in a steamer, cover, and steam over boiling water until tender, 4 to 6 minutes.
2. While carrots are steaming, stir butter and honey in a small saucepan over medium heat until the butter has melted.
3. Remove honey-butter mixture from heat and stir in parsley and lemon juice.
4. In a bowl, toss steamed carrots with honey-butter mixture until carrots are glazed.

Makes 4 servings

In the early sixties, when *Mary Poppins* (1964) was in production, Walt Disney approached his superstar songwriting team, Robert B. and Richard M. Sherman, about composing the music for an upcoming film about Winnie the Pooh. Their response was rather lackluster. "We were very uninterested in it to begin with, because we thought it was for kids," explains elder brother Richard. As it turned out, the two had never read the Milne stories, and it took an English colleague to indoctrinate them. Tony Walton, the design consultant for *Mary Poppins,* shared his stories about how he identified with the pudgy little bear who was "round, fat and proud of that," yet still managed to come out on top.

"The next thing we knew," says Robert, "we were kids again, thinking about Pooh as our friend." And the rest is music history.

The Sherman brothers wrote the songs for all four Pooh featurettes: *Winnie the Pooh and the Honey Tree* (1966), *Winnie the Pooh and the Blustery Day*

Right: Poster for Winnie the Pooh and the Honey Tree.

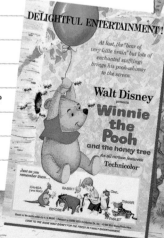

244

(1968), *Winnie the Pooh and Tigger Too* (1974), and *Winnie the Pooh and a Day for Eeyore* (1983). Also in 1983, they wrote many new songs for the new Disney Channel show *Welcome to Pooh Corner*, which featured a Puppetronics Pooh ensemble.

More Hundred-Acre Wood songs followed in the 1999 direct-to-video *Winnie the Pooh: Seasons of Giving*. The theatrical release of *The Tigger Movie* in 2000 marked the first time in nearly thirty years the

Sherman brothers teamed up on a Disney feature film, since the Oscar-nominated music for *Bedknobs & Broomsticks* (1971). That same year, Disney also released the "Sing Along" videos, *Sing a Song with Tigger* and *Sing a Song with Pooh Bear*, both of which landed on the top-ten best-seller charts for several weeks.

Above: (left to right) Richard M. Sherman, Wolfgang Reitherman, Robert B. Sherman, and composer Buddy Baker, 1966.

Over the years, the Sherman brothers have racked up a respectable laundry list of honors. Among them:

- 2 Academy Awards
- 9 Academy Award nominations
- 2 Grammy Awards
- 23 Gold and Platinum Certified albums
- 4 Golden Globe nominations
- Annie Award nomination
- Golden Laurel Award
- Star on Hollywood's Walk of Fame
- Disney Legends Award
- Broadcast Music, Incorporated Lifetime Acheivement Award

Left: Creating music for Winnie the Pooh and the Honey Tree. *Above: Robert B. Sherman* (left) *and Richard M. Sherman* (right) *visiting their star on the Hollywood Walk of Fame, May 1999.*

What's the Score

The Many Adventures of Winnie the Pooh (1981) includes all the songs Richard and Robert Sherman wrote for Disney's series of Pooh featurettes. With a little help from Pooh, who has already entered all the letters that spell his favorite food, can you identify the song titles?

Honey?

1.   _ _ nn _ e _he _ooh

2.   _ _, _ o _ n, _ n _ _ o _ _ h _ he _ _ o _ n _

3.   _ _ _ _ _ y _ n _ y _ _ _ _ _ y

4.   _ _ _ _ _ e _ _ _ _ _ _ _ _ n _ _ o _ _

5.   _ _ n _ o _ e _ _ _ _ _ e _

6.   _ _ _ _ he _ _ _ _ _ _ e _ y _ _ y

7.   _he _ on _ e _ _ _ _ _ h _ n _ _ _ o _ _ _ _ _ _ e _ _

8.   _he _ _ _ n, _ _ _ n, _ _ _ n _ _ _ e _ o _ n, _ o _ n, _ o _ n

9.   He _ _ _ _ _ _ _ _ _ n _ _ oo _ _ e _

10.   H _ _   H _ _   _ ooh- _ _ y

(Answers on page 351)

FACTS & FIGURES, TOO

■ Acreage of woodland of Ashdown Forest, the actual setting upon which A. A. Milne's stories are based: **6,400**

■ Acreage of woodland Winnie the Pooh and friends consider home: **100**

■ Amount E. P. Dutton Publishing Company insured original Christopher Robin toys (Pooh, Eeyore, Piglet, Kanga, and Tigger) for during a transatlantic tour from Great Britain to the United States in 1947: **$50,000**

■ Length of film, in feet, used for *Winnie the Pooh and the Honey Tree* : **1,995**

■ Number of pencils in millions used to sketch nearly 100,000 final drawings of characters in *Winnie the Pooh and the Honey Tree* (1966): **1,200,000**

■ Gallons of paint necessary to paint 32,000 celluloids for *Winnie the Pooh and the Honey Tree*: **423**

Retail value of teddy bears sold in the U.S. in 1999: **$2.7 billion**

■ Gallons of paint necessary to cover the White House: **570**

■ Number of Tiggers there would be if Tigger had a family tree: **more Tiggers than you could stick a shake at**

■ Fraction of teaspoon of honey a worker bee makes in her lifetime: **$1/12$**

■ U. S. annual per capita consumption of honey, in pounds: **1.1**

■ Pounds of honey required for an average bee colony to maintain itself for a year: **500**

■ Number of flowers a honeybee must tap into to produce one pound of honey: **2,000,000,000**

■ Number of flowers a honeybee must tap into to produce enough honey to support a Pooh Bear's daily diet of 12 (32 oz.) honeypots per year: **17,520,000,000,000**

ROO

One of the Hundred-Acre Wood's very small animals, Roo can often be found practicing his jumps in the Sandy Pit near his home. He is quite excitable by nature and always eager for a party or game of Pooh Sticks. His activities, however, are limited by his mother's insistence on nap times, mealtimes, and bath times. Roo is the only animal in the forest fortunate enough to have his own personal all-terrain vehicle for rapid transport (see Kanga).

HEIGHT: Pocket-sized; easily transportable. Considered by at least one bouncy forest animal as being on the smallish side of tiny and lacking in perpendicular.

SKIN: Water-resistant. Finds swimming as easy as falling into a river and slipping down a waterfall (and preferable to being bathed).

MOUTH: Claims to have a special method for simultaneously drinking milk and speaking. Although some (namely, Kanga) have disputed this ability, no one can deny Roo's talent for hiccuping.

HANDS: Excellent grip. Capable of latching onto a tigger's tail and rocking the forest.

TAIL: Versatile appendage. Can hang from, balance upon, swing with, and twist up like a corkscrew.

FEET: Good jumping skills. Has no problem keeping up with bouncier forest animals—very likely due to daily doses of strengthening medicine.

Strengthening Medicine

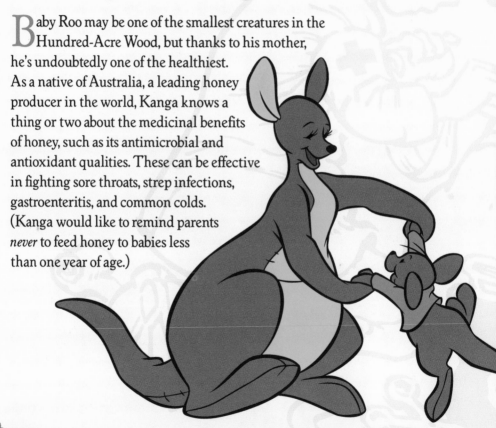

Baby Roo may be one of the smallest creatures in the Hundred-Acre Wood, but thanks to his mother, he's undoubtedly one of the healthiest. As a native of Australia, a leading honey producer in the world, Kanga knows a thing or two about the medicinal benefits of honey, such as its antimicrobial and antioxidant qualities. These can be effective in fighting sore throats, strep infections, gastroenteritis, and common colds. (Kanga would like to remind parents *never* to feed honey to babies less than one year of age.)

Lemon Honey Cold Blaster

1 cup boiling water
juice of two lemons
1 tablespoon honey

Add hot water to lemon juice and stir in honey until it dissolves. It does wonders to soothe sore throats and is packed with Vitamin C to fight off that cold.

Honey Grapefruit Soother

1 bag green tea
1 cinnamon stick
$1^1/_2$ cups boiling water
$1/_3$ cup grapefruit juice
4 teaspoons honey

In medium-sized teapot, place tea bag and cinnamon stick. Add boiling water and steep for three to five minutes. Remove tea bag and cinnamon stick and add grapefruit juice. Stir in honey until it dissolves. Pour into your favorite tea mug and sip away the winter sniffles.

Hot Milk 'n' Honey

8 ounces milk
1 tablespoon honey

Heat milk on stove top or in microwave. Stir in honey until dissolved. Serve warm just before bedtime to promote a good night's sleep. This age-old recipe has long been believed to be effective in curing constipation and bed-wetting.

Tummy-Calming Tea

1 bag fresh mint or chamomile tea
$1^1/_2$ cups boiling water
2 teaspoons honey

Place tea bag in medium-sized teapot and add boiling water. Steep for three to five minutes and remove tea bag. Add honey and stir. Served hot or cold, this drink is especially soothing for upset stomachs and achiness caused by gastroenteritis.

"No, Pooh, you don't eat them— you smell them."

In Which Pooh Has a Bath

Bath time has not always been Pooh's favorite activity. After all, Tigger lost his stripes from a bath once, and Piglet received a thoroughly unpleasant scrubbing because of a case of mistaken identity. But a dollop or two of sweetness added to the tub—or scrub—makes bath time almost as much fun as getting dirty.

Soothing Milk Bath

4 tablespoons powdered milk
2 tablespoons honey

Add ingredients to warm bathwater for a deliciously relaxing soak.

Daily Gentle Cleanser

1 teaspoon honey
1 teaspoon milk powder

Rub the honey and milk powder together in your palm for a non-irritating conditioning cleanser. Apply to your face and wash gently with warm water.

Vanilla Almond Foaming Bath

2 tablespoons honey
4 tablespoons almond oil
2 tablespoons mild liquid soap
1 teaspoon vanilla

Mix ingredients in small bowl and swirl into bathtub under running water to make a bubbly bath.

Sweet & Silky Hair Conditioner

2 tablespoons honey
1 tablespoon olive oil
1 or 2 drops essential oil of rosemary

Mix ingredients in small bowl. Work thoroughly into damp hair, massaging scalp as you do so. Wrap hair in warm towel and allow thirty minutes to condition. Shampoo gently and rinse with cool water.

Honey Citrus Scrub

2 tablespoons honey
4 tablespoons finely ground almonds
2 teaspoons grapefruit juice

Blend all ingredients together into a paste. Rub over skin as an exfoliating body wash, then rinse clean.

"Tigger"
Step-by-Step

THOUGH TIGGER'S HEA
STARTS WITH AN OV
IT HAS DEFINATE
FLATTENED
SURFACES.

THIS STRIPE ALSO
SERVES AS
EYEBROWS

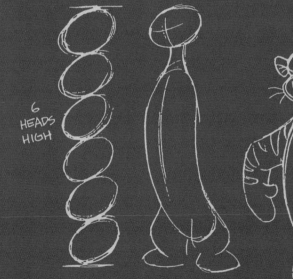

6 HEADS HIGH

KEEP TAIL ANGULAR AS
IF SPRING WAS COILED
INSIDE.

KEEP STRIPES
IRREGULAR IN SIZE
& SHAPE. USE THEM
TO HELP DEFINE BODY
CONTOURS

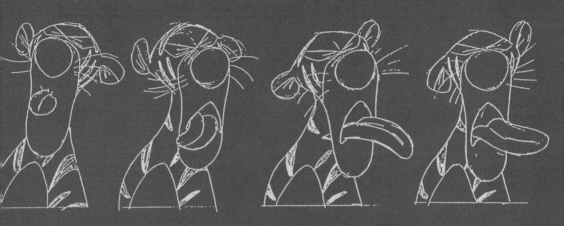

"TIGGER" AFTER TASTING SOMETHING HE <u>DIDN'T</u> LIKE!

Tigger Proof
Pumpkin Pie

When harvest season rolls around and your garden is overgrown with pumpkins, it's time to bake pumpkin pie. It shouldn't be partickerlerly surprising that the orange-ist inhabitant of the Hundred-Acre Wood has a recipe so easy and delicious you'll jump for joy, but if too many of the orange orbs get squashed by not-so-precise bouncing, canned pumpkins work just as nicely. For even more zing Tigger recommends adding jalapeños and tumeric (to taste).

FOR CRUST:

1 1/3 cups flour
1 tablespoon granulated sugar
1/4 teaspoon salt
1/2 stick (1/4 cup) sweet butter
1/4 cup vegetable shortening
2 tablespoons ice water

FOR PIE:

1 1/2 cups cooked or canned pumpkin
1/4 cup brown sugar
1/2 cup granulated sugar
1 1/2 cups condensed milk
1/4 teaspoon salt
1 teaspoon cinnamon
1 teaspoon ground ginger
1/4 teaspoon ground nutmeg
1/4 teaspoon ground cloves
2 eggs

1. Preheat oven to 425°F.
2. To make crust, sift together dry ingredients. In pastry blender or processor, cut in shortening and butter until mixture resembles coarse meal. Sprinkle water over dough and mix with fork until pastry is moist enough to form into a ball.
3. Roll out dough on lightly floured surface into a 14" round circle. Transfer and press into 9" pie pan. Trim overhang and crimp edges. Chill in freezer for 15 minutes.
4. To make the pumpkin filling, whisk all the pie ingredients together in large bowl until blended. Pour into the prepared crust.
5. Bake for 10 minutes, then lower oven temperature to 350°F and bake for an additional 40–50 minutes, or until knife inserted in center comes out clean.
6. Serve immediately with whipped cream!

Serves 8 to 10

THE
Tigger
MOVIE

TIDBITS

264

W hen *The Tigger Movie* hit the screens in the spring of 2000, it became the very first full-length animated feature starring the whole Hundred-Acre Wood gang. As seen in the title, the film shifts focus from the Willy-Nilly Ole Bear to the boisterous and bouncy Tigger, who realizes it can get a bit lonely being the only Tigger and sets out in search of his family. Some tiggerific tidbits:

■ Writer-Director Jun Falkenstein also directed the *Winnie the Pooh: Seasons of Giving* (1999) segment from "A Winnie the Pooh Thanksgiving" and the segment, "A Very Goofy Christmas" from *Mickey's Once Upon a Christmas* (1999).

■ *The Tigger Movie* artists worked simultaneously on the film in England, California, and Japan, with nearly 60 percent of the animation taking place at Walt Disney Animation in Japan.

■ Hidden Mickey hunters should keep a sharp eye out for falling snowflakes during the film's winter scenes.

■ Jim Cummings provided the voices for Tigger and Pooh. Cummings cites Paul Winchell, the original voice of Tigger, as his hero: "I got his book on how to be a ventriloquist when I was about nine years old and read it from cover to cover." Cummings has also brought to life Ed the hyena from *The Lion King* (1994), Darkwing Duck, and a host of film and television characters.

■ Richard M. and Robert B. Sherman, the chart-topping songwriting duo who composed all the songs for the original Winnie the Pooh films, teamed up again to write five new songs for *The Tigger Movie*.

A Treasure of Collectibles

The writer A. A. Milne purchased the very first Winnie the Pooh doll from the Harrods department store in London for his son's first birthday. The bear was made by the Alpha workshop of J. K. Farnell & Company, one of the first manufacturers to make teddy bears. The Alpha bears were made of Yorkshire mohair and soon became one of England's most popular teddies. That bear may have been the inspiration for the stories, but illustrator E. H. Shepard actually modeled his drawings after his own son's teddy, Growler, which was made by the German manufacturer, Steiff, the very first company to produce teddy bears at the turn of the twentieth century.

Within a few years of A. A. Milne's publication of *Winnie-the-Pooh* and *The House at Pooh Corner*, the silly old bear and his friends had already become an industry in England. Pooh admirers could buy spin-offs of the books, songbooks, calendars, greeting cards, games, dish sets, and, of course, toys.

Before Walt Disney acquired the rights to the A. A. Milne characters in the early 1960s, the most treasured items were dolls made by the Knickerbocker Toy Company and Agnes Brush.

Right: Christopher Robin rag doll by Gund.

With the Americanization of Winnie the Pooh came an entirely new look—and market—for the bear and his friends. The Gund Manufacturing Company was among the first licensees, and produced toys for Sears, Roebuck and Co., which had an exclusive arrangement with Disney to sell Pooh merchandise.

Prior to Disney's release of *Winnie the Pooh and the Honey Tree* (1966), Pooh merchandise was not produced in great quantities, which adds to the rarity and value of some of the earlier collectibles. Here's a look at some of the classics:

1940s–1950s

AGNES BRUSH

Created for sale at FAO Schwarz, Agnes Brush's 12-inch tall Winnie the Pooh wears a red cotton shirt with his initials stitched on the breast. Pooh is made of tan felt, and a 10-inch tall Piglet of cotton cloth. Both of their eyes are wooden.

Rabbit is made from tan and white felt, with eyes printed on the fabric. He wears a red ribbon around his neck and has white threads for whiskers. Eeyore's entire body is dark gray felt with a black yarn mane and tail tip. His eyes and mouth are stitched with black thread.

KNICKERBOCKER TOY COMPANY

Some of the earliest Knickerbocker Pooh bears wore atypical blue cotton shirts. Pooh measures 13 inches, and Piglet 11 inches. Piglet wears red-and-white-striped clothing that matches the insides of his ears. He's spruced up with a ribbon bowtie and black cotton feet. Both characters have black plastic eyes.

Eeyore, looking less doleful than usual, has a gray plush coat, a black yarn mane and tail, and black felt ears. He stands upright with help from wire reinforcements in his legs.

Roo is stuffed with wood chips (though not from the Hundred-Acre Wood!) and covered in peach corduroy fabric. Rabbit is also filled with wood chips and covered in yellow and white corduroy. The yellow-and-black-striped heffalump sports gauze wings shaped with wire.

1960s–1970s

GUND MANUFACTURING COMPANY

Some of these Pooh bears, sold in Sears stores, are made of polyester with black plastic noses and eyes. Others are in gold plush and wear red felt shirts. The 15-inch talking Pooh has a vocabulary of seven phrases, including "I'm Winnie the Pooh" and "You're my best friend."

Piglet wears a red-and-white-striped sewn-on cotton shirt and a red felt scarf around his neck that bears his name. Tigger comes in standing and sitting models, ranging from 7 to 20 inches in height. All are in orange-and-black-striped plush with white trim.

Eeyore is also available in numerous sizes, ranging from 8 to 13 inches high, with some floppier than others. Made of typical gray plush with black yarn manes, all have glued-on paper eyes.

R. JOHN WRIGHT

1980s

Many of Wright's toys were produced for sale at FAO Schwarz as well as The Disney Store and other retail outlets. Nearly all dolls are limited editions and have fully jointed limbs. Pooh comes in tan mohair and wears a maroon shirt, and Piglet, made of pink felt, wears a green-and-black-striped shirt. The Shepardesque Tigger is in black-and-mustard-striped felt. Eeyore, of course, is made of gray felt, and Kanga and Roo are both in brown plush. Christopher Robin

comes with an umbrella and raincoat. Pooh, Tigger, and Kanga all stand 8 inches tall. Eeyore is the largest at 18 inches and 3-inch Roo is the smallest, measuring two inches less than Piglet.

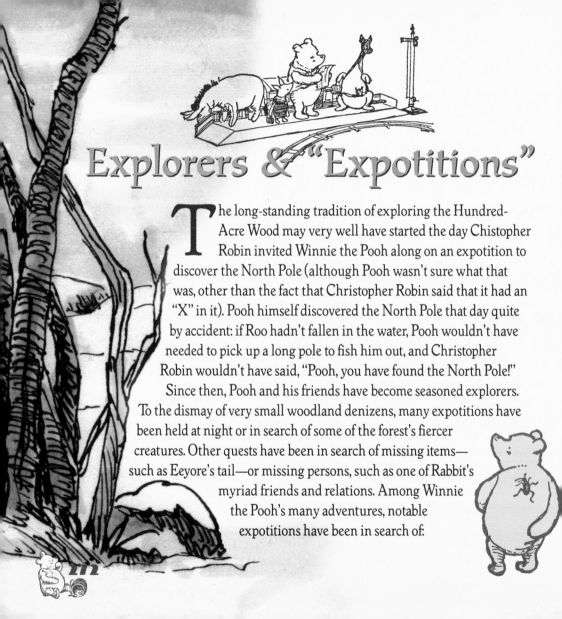

Explorers & "Expotitions"

The long-standing tradition of exploring the Hundred-Acre Wood may very well have started the day Chistopher Robin invited Winnie the Pooh along on an expotition to discover the North Pole (although Pooh wasn't sure what that was, other than the fact that Christopher Robin said that it had an "X" in it). Pooh himself discovered the North Pole that day quite by accident: if Roo hadn't fallen in the water, Pooh wouldn't have needed to pick up a long pole to fish him out, and Christopher Robin wouldn't have said, "Pooh, you have found the North Pole!" Since then, Pooh and his friends have become seasoned explorers. To the dismay of very small woodland denizens, many expotitions have been held at night or in search of some of the forest's fiercer creatures. Other quests have been in search of missing items—such as Eeyore's tail—or missing persons, such as one of Rabbit's myriad friends and relations. Among Winnie the Pooh's many adventures, notable expotitions have been in search of:

- Mist ... to lose Tigger
- Whatever-it-was that made tracks in the snow (quite possibly a woozle)
- The place where Tigger is, was, or should be
- Honey
- A treasure left behind by Owl's Great Uncle Waldo
- Gopher's helmet
- Piglet's lost shadow
- A turkey for Thanksgiving (believed to be among the fiercer creatures)
- Pooh's sweet tooth
- A bug (Christopher Robin's missing science experiment)
- Christopher Robin

273

THE
SEARCH FOR
CHRISTOPHER
ROBIN

On August 5, 1997, twenty years after the last Winnie the Pooh feature was produced, Disney released *Pooh's Grand Adventure: The Search for Christopher Robin* on video. Picking up where the previous stories left off, the adventure begins on the last day of a golden summer when Pooh and friends discover a mysterious note left by Christopher Robin. With some help from Owl, the woodland residents think that Christopher Robin is off to Skull—"a most forbidding and faraway place" ("school" to the rest of us.).

So Pooh, Piglet, Tigger, Rabbit, Eeyore, and Owl resolve to go on the quest of a lifetime to rescue him.

More than 150 individuals, including an international team of Disney's top artists, animators, and filmmakers, pooled their talents for more than two years to complete the long-awaited film. The hard work paid off: *Pooh's Grand Adventure* received five nominations for Annie Awards—one of the highest honors given for excellence in animation—in the areas of writing, directing, music, voice talent, and home video production.

Among the notable artists who contributed to the film are the musical performances of Kathy Lee Gifford, the masterful Paul Winchell as the voice of Tigger, Jim Cummings as the voice of Pooh, and Brady Bluhm as the voice of Christopher Robin.

Christopher Robin's Crossword

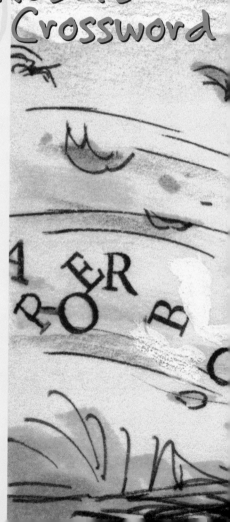

The real Christopher Robin loved crossword puzzles —a pastime he shared with his father, whose Sundays were not complete without the *London Times* crossword. Test your Hundred-Acre know-how below in the puzzle that even a bear of a little brain might get to the bottom of.

ACROSS
2. Name under which Pooh lives
8. Rain cloud alternate
9. One of the fiercer animals
10. Blustery day
11. Handy bellpull or little bit of extra

DOWN
1. Kite string?
3. Sort of surprise
4. Loud cough (for some)
5. Honey bandit
6. Where Roo plays
7. Unfavorable atmospheric conditions

(Answers on page 351)

KANGA

In the northwest corner of the Hundred-Acre Wood, right next to the Sandy Pit where Roo plays, is where you'll find Kanga's House. Although something of an exotic newcomer, Kanga came to the woods in "the Usual Way," according to Christopher Robin. First and foremost, Kanga is a mother and brings her motherly ways to all the animals in the woods. She is the ultimate reminder of manners, bedtimes, bath times, and mealtimes.

EARS: Acute hearing with special ability to tune out particular frequencies—i.e., Owl's rendition of long words that include "encyclopedia" and "rhododendron."

EYES: Keen eyesight that detects the difference between a flying Piglet and a flying kite.

HANDS: Medicine dispensers and multipurpose scrubbers. Especially useful for washing family members with extra soap (or dirty Piglets disguising themselves as dirty family members).

POUCH: A pocket for carrying family members—namely Baby Roo (and, on occasion, other very small animals, such as Piglet).

FEET: Large feet that make Kanga one of the fastest runners (and jumpers) in the woods. Although she is unquestionably faster than Rabbit, Kanga knows that her jumps do not compare to Tigger's bounces.

279

KANGA'S
Beauty Secrets

Although Kanga has been mistaken for one of the forest's fiercer animals, the only things she might possibly be fierce about would be Roo's bedtimes or guarding her well-kept beauty secrets. Most woodland denizens recognize Kanga as a very hard-working mother who knows the importance of good care and proper pampering. But what the others may not know is that Kanga takes the time to pamper herself, too. She relies on one essential spa ingredient that has the ability to retain moisture and soothe sensitive skin as well as provide a natural antiseptic, exfoliant, and antioxidant. If Winnie the Pooh knew that his favorite food did all that, Pooh might turn Kanga's beauty lotions into his breakfast notions.

Soothing Skin Softener

1 teaspoon honey
1 teaspoon almond oil
1/4 teaspoon lemon juice

Blend ingredients together and rub into dry skin. Allow skin to soak up moisture for 10 minutes, then rinse off excess with warm water. Especially good for dry elbows and heels.

Skin-Firming Mask

1 tablespoon honey
1 egg white
1 teaspoon glycerin
4–6 tablespoons flour

Whisk ingredients into a smooth paste. Spread over face and throat with finger-tips in small, upward circular motions and leave on for 10 to 15 minutes. Rinse with warm water.

Milk & Honey Moisture Mask

2 tablespoons honey
2 teaspoons milk

Blend ingredients, then gently smooth over your face and throat. Leave on for 10 minutes and rinse with warm water.

Refreshing Honey Apple Toner

1 apple, peeled and cored
1 tablespoon honey

Puree ingredients. Apply to cleansed skin and relax for 15 minutes. Rinse face with cool water and gently pat dry.

Deep-Cleaning Mask

1/4 cup honey
1/2 cup oatmeal

Mix ingredients together into paste. Apply generously onto face as a thick mask and leave on for thirty minutes. Rinse off with warm water.

TV: Pooh's New Look

More than twenty-five years before The Walt Disney Company aired its first cable program based on Winnie the Pooh, NBC had acquired the rights to create a television show about the silly old bear. The network planned a show but in 1960 decided not to proceed with the property. The following year, Walt Disney bought the rights from NBC. With the notable exception of several 1970s television specials that aired the Pooh theatrical featurettes, Winnie the Pooh did not have a regular television presence until 1983. Since then, Pooh Bear has continued to have quite a run on the airwaves.

WELCOME TO POOH CORNER

THE NEW ADVENTURES OF WINNIE THE POOH (*1988–1993; 1995–1996*)

This animated series got its start on Disney Channel in January 1988, then moved into ABC's Saturday morning lineup in the fall of that year. The show was an immediate success and garnered numerous honors, including two Emmys, a Parent's Choice Award, an Action for Children's Television Award, and a Humanitas Award.

THE BOOK OF POOH (*2001–present*)

A new incarnation of Pooh and friends debuted on Disney Channel's *Playhouse Disney* in January 2001. The live-action show is inspired by a 300-year-old Japanese art form called bunraku puppetry. Geared toward preschoolers, *The Book of Pooh* promotes a whole child curriculum that includes reading readiness, a love of books, and social and cognitive development.

WELCOME TO POOH CORNER

(*1983–1995*) Pooh and friends helped launch The Disney Channel cable television network in 1983 and remained a network staple for twelve years. The innovative show featured life-sized puppets based on A. A. Milne's characters. An advanced electronic circuitry system called Puppetronics enabled the humans to manipulate facial gestures and expressions from within the costumes. The Sherman brothers, longtime Pooh composers, wrote many new songs for the series, which featured lessons on safety or morals.

THE BOOK OF POOH

Pooh's Puppet Masters

For the newest incarnation of Winnie the Pooh, Disney artists combined an ancient Japanese art form with modern technology. The result: the Disney Channel series, *The Book of Pooh*, which is the first television program to blend bunraku puppetry with computer-generated virtual sets. Emmy Award–winning executive producer Mitchell Kriegman wanted "to do something that went to the root of Pooh, which was the physicality of the characters," and bunraku puppetry was a natural choice.

The bunraku puppet theater brings

together the Japanese art forms of stylized narrative storytelling (*joruri*), puppet manipulation (*ningyo*), and musical accompaniment (*shamisen*) that provide atmosphere and sound effects. The essential elements of bunraku originated in Japan as early as the fifteenth and sixteenth centuries, and by the seventeenth century became a unified, recognized art form.

The bunraku style of puppetry generally requires three to five puppeteers working in synchronous unison to handle a single puppet: one controls the head and right arm, one the left arm, and a third the feet. The puppets are about half the size of the humans guiding them, which enables the puppeteers to manipulate eyebrows, mouths, and hands with surprisingly lifelike and graceful gestures. Onstage, as seen in *The Lion King* on Broadway, the puppeteers are visible to the audience. But in *The Book of Pooh*, Kriegman erased the puppeteers with groundbreaking computer-generated animation and then superimposed the puppets onto a virtual background.

For a whole new generation, *The Book of Pooh* brings Pooh and his friends to life in an entirely new way, leaving more than one viewer to say, "It's a *real* Pooh!"

The Book of Pooh

EEYORE

In the southeast corner of the Hundred-Acre Wood, don't expect to find the usual rolling hills, wooded forests, and bubbling brooks. There, the land is cold, boggy, sad, and rather thistly. It is just the sort of place only a gloomy donkey could love, which is why it has come to be known as Eeyore's Gloomy Place. When Eeyore isn't dining on thistles, he usually can be found entangled in house renovations. Although most of his friends consider him a rather glum chum, Eeyore has on occasion worn party hats and eaten cake.

288

BODY: Can double as a floating device (important in the event of getting bounced in the water by Tigger).

HEAD: Has a brain. Is one of the few Hundred-Acre Wood animals capable of thought (even if the thoughts are ominous and dismal).

EARS: Occasionally hard of hearing. Can push ear forward to improve reception, especially when very small animals mention they've brought him a birthday present.

EYES: Able to search for small things (such as friends and relations of Rabbit's) for several days without eye strain (even after others forget to tell him to stop looking).

MOUTH: Adapted to eating gorse bushes and thistles. Prickly diet may have influence on behavior.

HOOF: Special ability to drop sticks in a "twitchy" kind of way when playing Pooh Sticks.

TAIL: Sometimes known as "the little bit of extra at the back." Detachable. (Can be reattached with hammer and nail.)

A Storyboard for Eeyore

When animation writers Steve Hulett, Pete Young, Ron Clements, and Tony L. Marino got together to create a new Winnie the Pooh featurette, they spent hours watching the first three Pooh films and reading A. A. Milne's stories before settling on the lone inhabitant of the Gloomy Place. "Eeyore has always been one of our most popular characters," says Young, yet he never had a starring role in any of the previous films. *Winnie the Pooh and a Day for Eeyore* (1983) gave the morose donkey his due. For the adaptation, they chose the Milne stories "In Which Eeyore Has a Birthday and Gets Two Presents" and "Pooh Invents a New Game and Eeyore Joins In."

DID SOMEBODY PUSH YOU?

SOMEBODY BOUNCED ME

But the process was not a simple one. "Some of what Milne wrote doesn't translate to the screen," says Hulett. "A story will go on for half a page telling you what a character is thinking. And while that's great and amusing on the printed page, it doesn't always work in a visual sense." They resolved these problems in the storyboarding

EEYORE? COULD YO STOP TURNING 'R FOR A MOMENT

AND, UH... I HAPPENED TO
BEHIND EEYORE... AND... AN

(POOH O.S.)
...USE IT MUDDLES
RATHER.

I LIKE TURNING 'ROUND.

process. Young and Clements sketched out scene after scene, while Hulett and Marino adapted the dialogue. After necessary juggling, cutting, viewing, and reviewing, Eeyore would finally get his day.

...S THINKING BY THE ...OF THE RIVER, MINDING...

...MY OWN BUSINESS, WHEN I RECEIVED A LOUD BOUNCE-

(POOH)
BUT WHO DID IT?

(TIGGER)
...ND...I SAID...

GRRRRR...

...ROOOOPTSCHSLTZ!!!

...nd a Day for Eeyore

THE HUNDRED-ACRE WOOD BOASTED many natural wonders, but none was more beautiful than a tiny stream running through the forest. By the time this stream reached the edge of the forest, it was almost a river. And crossing the river at its most peaceful spot was an old wooden bridge. It was a familiar spot to Winnie the Pooh, for he would often wander down there, doing nothing in particular and thinking nothing in particular. But on the most recent of these excursions, something took his mind off nothing.

PLOP! A pinecone fell out of a tree and landed right on Pooh's head. "Hmm," he said, picking it up. "This is a very good fir cone, and something ought to rhyme with it. Think, think, think." While Pooh was thinking about a poem, a gentle breeze sent him tumbling down the path all the way to the old wooden bridge. And Pooh's pinecone tumbled—*SPLASH!*—into the water below.

"Oh bother. I suppose I shall have to find another one." Pooh sighed. He looked down at the water below and saw his pinecone drifting away. "That's funny, I dropped it on the other side and it came out on this side. Hmm." Pooh hurried off and gathered a whole armful of pinecones. He picked out two and dropped them in the water on one side of the bridge, then ran to the other side. The big one came out first, and the little one came out last. And that was the beginning of a game Pooh invented called Pooh Sticks. Pooh decided to call it Pooh Sticks instead of Pooh Cones because sticks were easier to collect.

One day, Pooh and Piglet, Rabbit and Roo were all on the bridge, playing Pooh Sticks together. *SPLASH!* Everyone's sticks fell in the water and Pooh, Piglet, Rabbit, and Roo rushed to the other side of the bridge. The tip of something dark emerged from under the bridge.

"Eeyore!" everyone shouted.

"Eeyore! What are you doing down there?" asked Rabbit.

"Give you three guesses," said Eeyore.

"Fishing?" Pooh guessed.

"Going for a sail?" offered Roo.

"Wrong," said Eeyore.

Rabbit tried a guess. "Waiting for somebody to, uh, help you out of the river?"

"That's right." Eeyore said flatly.

"I've got an idea," suggested Pooh. "If we all throw stones and things into the river on one side of Eeyore, the stones would make waves and the waves would wash him to the other side." Pooh disappeared and soon returned with a very, very large rock. He leaned over the rail and dropped the stone right in the middle of . . . Eeyore! The poor donkey disappeared under a big splash.

"Oh dear!" said Pooh sadly. "Perhaps it wasn't such a very good idea, after all."

But Roo spotted Eeyore climbing onto the riverbank. "There he is!" shouted Roo.

Everyone gathered around the riverbank.

Above: Eeyore waits patiently to be rescued. Storyboard art.

"How did you fall in, Eeyore?" Rabbit wanted to know.

"I was bounced," said Eeyore matter-of-factly.

"Eeyore, was it—?" Before Rabbit could finish his sentence he found himself suddenly and violently bounced to the ground.

"Tigger!" Rabbit shouted.

"Hello, Rabbit!" greeted Tigger bouncily.

Rabbit sat up and put his hands on his hips. "Tigger, what happened just now," he demanded.

"Just when?" asked Tigger innocently.

"When you bounced Eeyore into the river," said Rabbit.

"Oh," said Tigger sheepishly. "I didn't bounce him."

"He bounced me," Eeyore confirmed.

"No!" Tigger protested. "I didn't, really! Well, I . . . I just had a cough, you see, and I happened to be behind Eeyore and I said . . . that . . . I said, 'GRRRR . . . ROOOOPTSCHSLTZ!!!' Hoo-ho-ho-HOO!"

Well, it turned out that when Eeyore was thinking by the side of the river, Tigger really did bounce him. "Yeah, well, it was just a joke," Tigger insisted. And with that, he bounced off.

 298

Preceding pages: Eeyore, bounced. Production still.

"Tigger's so thoughtless with his bouncing," Rabbit scolded.

"Why should Tigger think of me?" moped Eeyore. "Nobody else does."
Eeyore sighed and then ambled away back to his gloomy spot.

A worried Pooh found his donkey friend getting rained on underneath his very own rain cloud. "Eeyore? What's the matter?" asked Pooh. "You seem so sad."

"Why should I be sad?" said Eeyore . "It's my birthday. The happiest day of the year."

"Oh! Well, many happy returns of the day, Eeyore," Pooh said cheerily.

"Thank you, Pooh." Eeyore said. "But we can't all, and some of us don't."

"Can't all what?" asked Pooh, confused.

"No gaiety," Eeyore droned. "No song and dance. No 'Here we go round the mulberry bush.' But don't worry about me, Pooh. Go and enjoy yourself. I'll stay here and be miserable." Eeyore moped. "With no presents, no cake, no candles."

Suddenly, Pooh had an idea. "Eeyore! Wait right here." Pooh hurried home as fast as he could when who should he find in front of his house but … "Piglet!"

"I found out what's troubling poor Eeyore," he told Piglet. "It's his birthday, and nobody has taken any notice of it." Pooh went in and looked around his house. "Hmm. I must get poor Eeyore a present of some sort." Then his eyes fell upon the answer. "Honey! That should do very well. What are you going to give, Piglet?" he asked his friend.

"Perhaps I could give Eeyore a balloon," Piglet thought. "I have one at home!"

So, off Piglet trotted in one direction, and in the other direction went Pooh with his jar of honey. However, Pooh hadn't gone very far when a very funny feeling began to creep over him ... as if someone inside him were saying, "Now then, Pooh, time for a little something."

Pooh decided to have a little something. And then he had a little more. And a little more. Until he had taken his last lick from the inside of the jar.

"Now, let me see," said Pooh with a honey-smeared face. "Where was I going? Oh yes, Eeyore. I was going to—" Suddenly, Pooh looked in his empty honeypot.

"Oh bother! I must give Eeyore something." Right about then, Pooh looked up and saw that he had come upon Owl's house. "I think I shall go see my good friend Owl," he decided.

"Many happy returns of Eeyore's birthday, Owl," greeted Pooh. "I'm giving Eeyore this useful pot to keep things in and I wanted to ask you . . . ." started Pooh.

"A useful pot?" said Owl. "Hoo! You ought to write 'happy birthday' on it."

"That was what I wanted to ask you," said Pooh. "My spelling is wobbly."

"Hmm, very well then." Owl put on his spectacles and contemplated Pooh's useful pot for a moment before he started writing. "There," Owl announced.

"Thank you, Owl. Eeyore will be most pleased," said Pooh.

"Ooh, I hope so! Ooh, this is so exciting. I'm flying directly over to Christopher Robin's to tell him the news!" At once, Owl took flight high over the Hundred-Acre Wood, where far down below he saw Piglet running with a big red balloon. "Many happy returns of Eeyore's birthday, Piglet!" Owl hooted from above.

"And many happy returns to you, too, Owl!" Piglet looked up to see Owl, and as he did, he ran directly into a tree! Then poor Piglet and his balloon bounced

Preceding pages: "I must get poor Eeyore a present of some sort. . . honey!"
Storyboard art. Right: Owl's house sits on top of an old beech tree. Storyboard art.

quite a ways down the road until ... *BANG!* All Piglet was left with was a popped balloon. So, with droopy ears, little Piglet made his way to Eeyore's gloomy spot with his broken gift.

Piglet found Eeyore moping under a tree. "Many happy returns of the d-d-d-day," offered Piglet as cheerily as he could. "I ... I brought you a present!"

Eeyore's ears perked up. "Pardon me, Piglet, my hearing must be going. I thought you said you brought me a present."

"I did," Piglet said directly in Eeyore's ear. "I brought you a b-b-ba-balloon," said Piglet sadly. "But I'm afraid ... oh, I'm very sorry, but when I was running— that is, to bring it, I fell down and ...."

"My balloon? My birthday balloon?" said Eeyore.

Right about then, Pooh arrived. "Many happy returns of the day, Eeyore!

Left: Piglet runs through the Hundred-Acre Wood with a big red balloon. Storyboard art.

I brought you a little present. It's a useful pot. And it's got 'A very happy birthday with love from Pooh' written on it. And it's for putting things in."

"Like a balloon," said Eeyore.

Pooh shook his head. "Oh no, Eeyore. Balloons are much too big to go in a . . . ."

But Eeyore had already picked up the burst balloon in his teeth and dropped it into the pot. "So it *does*," said Pooh.

Eeyore couldn't stop smiling as he dropped his bit of balloon in and out and in and out of his useful pot.

That afternoon, Christopher Robin, Rabbit, Roo, Kanga, Pooh, Piglet, and Owl threw a party for Eeyore and cheered as he blew out all the candles on his birthday cake. Suddenly, Tigger appeared and bounced Rabbit to the ground.

Rabbit was not amused. "You've got a lot of nerve showing up here after what you did to Eeyore. Hmph! I think Tigger should leave," said Rabbit defiantly.

"Aw, let him stay," pleaded Roo. Tigger nodded in agreement.

Pooh knew the right person to ask. "What do you think, Christopher Robin?"

And, of course, Christopher Robin had the right answer. "I think, I think we all ought to . . . play Pooh Sticks!"

So they gathered on the old wooden bridge and played the game for many contented hours. And Eeyore, who had never played it before, won more times than anyone else. But poor Tigger won none at all.

"Tiggers don't like Pooh Sticks," Tigger growled when it was time for everyone to go home. He threw down his stick and walked off with no bounce at all.

Eeyore followed Tigger. "Tigger, I'd be happy to tell you my secret for winning at Pooh Sticks," said the birthday donkey.

"You would?" said Tigger, brightening.

"It's very easy," explained Eeyore. "You just have to let your stick drop in a twitchy sort of way."

"I forgot to twitch! That was my problem!" Tigger was so excited that he bounced right into Eeyore. Again.

Meanwhile, Christopher Robin, Pooh, and Piglet stayed awhile on the bridge, enjoying the lazy afternoon. "Tigger's all right, really," Piglet said. "Of course, he is," said Christopher Robin.

"Everybody is, really," said Pooh. "That's what I think. But I don't suppose I'm right."

"Of course you are," Christopher Robin laughed. "Silly old bear!" ∎

Right: They played Pooh Sticks for many contented hours. Storyboard art.

Candles and Pink Sugar

For some, the happiest day of the year includes a little song and dance or game of "Here We Go Round the Mulberry Bush." For others, like Eeyore—who remarks about happiness that "we can't all, and some of us don't"—the best ingredients for a birthday add up to a slice of cake with pink frosting.

FOR CAKE:
2 1/4 cups sifted white flour
3 teaspoons baking powder
1/2 teaspoon salt
4 ounces unsweetened baker's chocolate
1 stick (1/2 cup) butter
1 1/4 cups granulated sugar
1 cup milk
1 1/2 teaspoons vanilla
1/2 teaspoon almond extract
4 egg whites (room temparature)

FOR FROSTING:
1 stick (1/2 cup) butter
2 cups confectioners' sugar
3 tablespoons milk
1 teaspoon vanilla
red food coloring

1. Preheat oven to 350°F. Line two 9-inch round pans with lightly greased wax paper, greased side up.
2. Combine flour, baking powder, and salt and sift into medium-sized bowl; set aside.
3. In double boiler, melt chocolate.
4. In large bowl, cream butter and sugar together until light and fluffy.
5. Combine milk, vanilla, almond extract, and melted chocolate. Add to butter-sugar mixture in three stages, alternating with sifted ingredients. Beat until smooth after each addition.

6. In separate bowl, whip egg whites until stiff, but not dry. Fold into cake batter.

7. Pour batter evenly into cake pans and bake for 25 minutes, or until toothpick comes out clean. Cool on wire rack.

8. To make frosting, cream butter and confectioners' sugar together. Beat in milk and vanilla until smooth. Add a few drops of food coloring and stir until desirable shade of pink is reached. *Tip: To thicken, add more confectioners' sugar; to thin, add more milk.*

9. Place one cake layer on platter and spread top with frosting. Place second cake layer on top of first and frost top and sides.

10. Top your cake with candles and your guests with party hats, and let the gaiety begin!

Serves 8 to 10

Eeyore's Uses for a Useful Pot

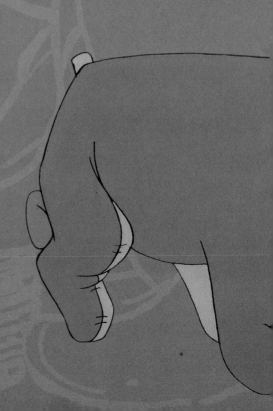

Once, Pooh found a pot of honey and asked Eeyore if it belonged to him. "It isn't mine," he replied, adding, "Then again, few things are." But ever since the day Pooh accidentally ate all the honey that he'd planned to give Eeyore for his birthday and gave him the empty honeypot instead, Eeyore has had a useful place in which to put the few things that *are* his:

- Birthday balloons (only if popped)
- Thistles
- Extra bow (for tail)
- Extra pin (to reattach tail, if necessary)
- Tail (to prevent it from getting lost)
- A bit of string (you never know when it might be useful)
- Violets picked by a very small animal
- A box of paints from Christopher Robin
- A flower (or a Piglet disguised like one)
- A good stick

VOICES OF THE WOOD

POTATO GIVES VOICE TO RABBIT

When Walt Disney was searching the Hollywoods to find an actor to give voice to Rabbit, one of the delightful characters in his newest animated-cartoon featurette, *Winnie the Pooh and the Honey Tree*, he recalled an actor who once played a potato on radio.

"Get me Junius Matthews," Walt urged his casting office. "Anyone who can personalize a potato should be good for Rabbit."

And so Junius, with extensive stage, screen, radio, and television experience has turned himself into a rabbit with the voice of a hot potato and set up some of the funniest scenes in the picture.

STERLING HOLLOWAY GIVES VOICE TO WINNIE THE POOH

When Winnie the Pooh is given voice for the first time in Walt Disney's enchanting animated-cartoon featurette, *Winnie the Pooh and the Honey Tree*, it will be Sterling Holloway speaking for one of the most famous and beloved characters in children's literature.

With a voice that's as stretchy as a rubber band, he provides speech for more than 20 Disney characters, including a car, a house, and a hot stove, as well as assorted animals.

POOH CHARACTERS IN PERFECT VOICE FOR WALT DISNEY CARTOON FILM DEBUT

Howard Morris, for several seasons a regular on Steve Allen's television show and now one of Hollywood's most sought-after movie and TV comedians, makes his Disney debut as the voice of the gopher. This delightful addition to the Hundred-Acre Wood makes his own debut, explaining his presence by exclaiming, "I'm not in the book, you know!"

That fine performer of stage, screen, and television, Sebastian Cabot, handles the off-scene narration. The son of a London photographer, Cabot left an apprenticeship to a chef while in his teens to follow an acting career, having discovered his penchant for mimicry and dialects. Last heard as the bombastic Sir Ector in Disney's recent animated-cartoon success, *The Sword in the Stone*, Cabot is currently voicing the role of Bagheera, the panther, for Walt's upcoming cartoon feature, *The Jungle Book*.

Barbara Luddy, who for a number of years was the star of radio's perennial favorite, *The Chicago Theatre of the Air*, and who voiced the role of Lady in *Lady and the Tramp*, speaks for Kanga. A sudden voice change forced Barbara to abandon a flourishing career as a child musical comedy star and try her luck in nonsinging roles. The husky vocal quality she acquired soon became an asset and opened up a whole new career for her. Radio

became Barbara's forte and she created more than 1,000 roles over the airwaves.

TIGGER IS FEATURED IN NEW POOH

He wears striped pajamas, bounces a lot, and tends to speak in initials. His name is Tigger, which he spells "T-I-double-Guh-Rrr," and he is the striped star of Walt Disney's *Winnie the Pooh and the Blustery Day*. With the unique vocal talents of Paul Winchell, Tigger uses a manner of speech which endears him to audiences.

Actor-ventriloquist Winchell got his start with a couple of dummies named Jerry Mahoney and Knucklehead Smiff. They starred in their own television series until 1957, when Winchell left show business to spend three years at Columbia University studying medicine. As an apprentice intern at Columbia, Winchell invented new surgical tools and appliances, including an artificial heart, which he patented in 1961.

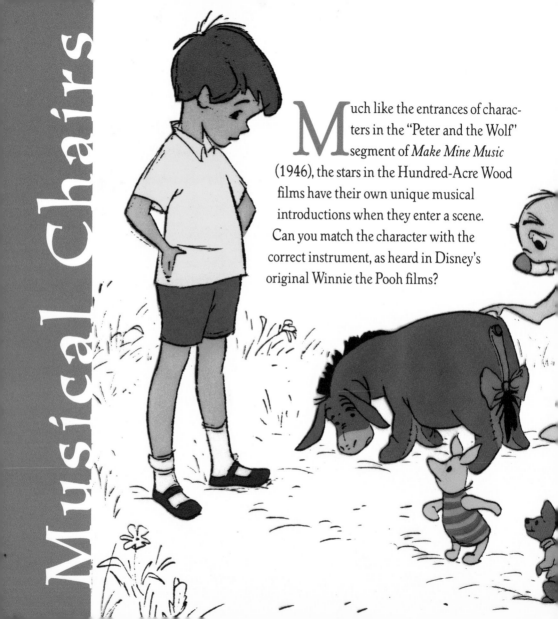

Musical Chairs

Much like the entrances of characters in the "Peter and the Wolf" segment of *Make Mine Music* (1946), the stars in the Hundred-Acre Wood films have their own unique musical introductions when they enter a scene. Can you match the character with the correct instrument, as heard in Disney's original Winnie the Pooh films?

1. __ Christopher Robin   a. Flute

2. __ Eeyore   b. Oboe

3. __ Gopher   c. Baritone horn

4. __ Kanga   d. Clarinet

5. __ Owl   e. Bass harmonica

6. __ Piglet   f. Piccolo

7. __ Pooh   g. Trumpet and guitar

8. __ Rabbit   h. Ocarina and French horn

9. __ Roo   i. Bass clarinet

(Answers on page 351)

319

Unlike most heroes of children's stories, Winnie the Pooh, Piglet, Eeyore, Kanga, and Roo started out as stuffed animals before having countless adventures as fictional characters. Christopher Robin may have been the first owner of Hundred-Acre Wood plush toys, but only the first of millions. When Walt Disney released the first animated Pooh film in 1965, American children quickly became familiar with the British bear, thanks to a comprehensive marketing program with Sears, Roebuck and Co. That year also saw major promotional tie-ins with Nabisco and McCall's as well as licensed merchandise from 30 major manufacturers. Since then, Pooh merchandise continues to be an ever-growing phenomenon. Here's a peek at how Pooh and his friends became part of our national consumer consciousness:

■ *McCall's* magazine December 1965 issue advertised McCall's pattern #8087. For 50 cents, crafty moms could buy the plans for a pink cotton Piglet in an orange-and-pink-striped shirt, a gold terry-cloth Pooh in his signature red shirt, and Kanga with Baby Roo in brown cotton.

■ Sears published 11 million Spring '66 catalogs featuring page after page of children's wear, infants' wear, children's bedding, and stuffed animals, all based on the Winnie the Pooh theme.

Beginning January 1, 1966, Nabisco advertised a "hunny of an offer" in 4 million boxes of Rice Honeys and Wheat Honeys cereals. Each of the special boxes contained a free Breakfast Buddy—a tiny figure of Winnie the Pooh, Christopher Robin, Kanga, Roo, Owl, Rabbit, Piglet, and Eeyore. The arms of the Breakfast Buddies hooked onto cereal bowls, spoons, and pencils.

Twenty-one cities celebrated "Winnie the Pooh Week." Special events included a Winnie the Pooh Tea Party, Pooh Tour Group visitations at local hospital children's wards, benefit fashion shows, and Grandmother's Day at Sears, where the Hundred-Acre Wood characters were present.

Pooh, Eeyore, Owl, Rabbit, Kanga, and Roo traveled across the country via the Disney plane as part of a personal appearance tour. In each city, big brass bands, fan clubs, and the press greeted the characters.

In addition to books published by E. P. Dutton and Golden Press, Whitman Publishing Company offered numerous Pooh products in 1965. They included books, coloring books, sticker fun, frame tray puzzles, and activity sets that retailed for 29 cents to $1.

Eeyore's Birthday, TEXAS STYLE

For one doleful donkey, there's no more need to be sad and gloomy about friends' forgetting his birthday. Every year around the middle of April, the folks in Austin, Texas, hold a massive birthday party celebration to honor Eeyore.

Eeyore's Birthday Party was the brainchild of a group of University of Texas graduate English majors led by Lloyd W. Birdwell Jr. and James Ayers. It all started in 1963 with a "May Day meets Woodstock"—type daylong event at the university. The bohemian rite-of-spring party drew hundreds of hippies for a day of costumes, drum circles, maypole dancing, acoustic music, and, of course, birthday cake. The guest of honor: a live gray donkey.

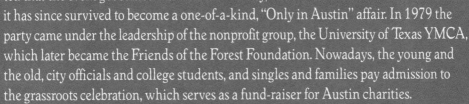

In the years that followed, party organizers admitted that the event got somewhat wild and woolly, but it has since survived to become a one-of-a-kind, "Only in Austin" affair. In 1979 the party came under the leadership of the nonprofit group, the University of Texas YMCA, which later became the Friends of the Forest Foundation. Nowadays, the young and the old, city officials and college students, and singles and families pay admission to the grassroots celebration, which serves as a fund-raiser for Austin charities.

In 2001, Eeyore's Birthday Party-goers made contributions possible to thirteen local charities, including AnimalKind Foundation, Inc., which assists abandoned animals; Hospice Austin, for terminally ill patients; SafePlace Austin, which provides support to abused women and children; and DiverseArts, for local music and art festivals.

A Not-So-Gloomy Gus

Eyore's melancholy nature has been misunderstood at one time or another by just about every creature in the Hundred-Acre Wood. Most consider him a dour, sad, and pessimistic donkey who spends a lot of time under rain clouds feeling sorry for himself. But, in truth, Eyore has a good sense of humor, maintains a practical outlook, and is always ready to help his friends in need.

In his own special way, Eeyore likes to:

■ Cheer up friends. When Tigger wishes he could hear from members of his family tree, Eeyore advises him to keep smiling.

■ Give credit where credit is due. When Rabbit guesses correctly what Eeyore is doing in the river, he says, "Give Rabbit the time and he'll get the answer."

■ Be gracious. When others take note of him, he says, "Thanks for noticing."

■ Catch friends by surprise with a little joke. On birthdays, the seemingly grim donkey is especially good at tricking others into thinking he's surrounded by cake and presents.

■ Look on the bright side. When it's freezing in Eeyore's gloomy corner of the wood and the snow is still snowing, at least there hasn't been an earthquake lately.

■ Think of others first. When Eeyore's tail gets cold and numb, if nobody minds, then it's all right.

■ Take a no-nonsense approach. In the case of Owl's fallen tree house, Eeyore observed, "When your house looks like that, it's time to find another one."

■ Assume the best. When Owl flies overhead and notices him but doesn't say anything, Eeyore still finds it friendly and encouraging.

■ Offer simple explanations. "Getting wet is something that happens to you when you've been in the river for a long time."

Eeyore's Thistle Salad with Honey Dressings

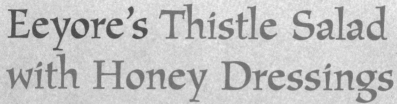

When asked to bring a favorite dish for potluck dinners or holidays, Pooh naturally brings honey, whereas Eeyore is sure to bring enough thistles for everyone at the table. As Pooh has learned, prickly things are best enjoyed when not sat upon. And with a little honey, the heart of *Cynara cardunculus*, commonly known as artichoke thistle, can be quite tasty with the proper preparations. You can usually find marinated hearts of the less prickly variety at your local grocery store.

FOR SALAD, TOSS:
6 cups shredded romaine lettuce or
mixed greens
1 cup cherry tomatoes, halved
6 ounces marinated artichoke hearts,
drained
freshly grated Parmesan cheese, to taste

Top with one of the following dressings:

Honey-Balsamic Vinaigrette
Combine $1/3$ cup balsamic vinegar, 1 tablespoon honey, 1 teaspoon minced garlic, and 1 teaspoon minced fresh ginger.

Honey-Mustard Vinaigrette
Combine 2 tablespoons honey, 2 tablespoons Dijon mustard, 1 teaspoon ginger, 2 tablespoons red wine vinegar, 1 teaspoon soy sauce, 1 teaspoon minced garlic, and 1 tablespoon minced fresh chives with $1/2$ cup olive oil.

Spicy Honey-Orange Dressing
Combine $1/3$ cup fresh orange juice, 2 tablespoons fresh lime juice, 1 tablespoon minced onion, 2 teaspoons honey, $1/2$ teaspoon ground cumin, $1/4$ teaspoon salt, and $1/4$ teaspoon black pepper with $1/2$ cup vegetable oil.

Creamy Honey-Shallot Dressing
Blend 2 tablespoons honey, 2 tablespoons minced shallots, 2 tablespoons red wine vinegar, and $1/4$ teaspoon paprika with $1/2$ cup mayonnaise.

Herbed Honey Vinaigrette
Combine $1/3$ cup white wine vinegar, $1/3$ cup honey, 3 tablespoons fresh chopped basil, and 1 tablespoon minced green onion. Add salt and pepper to taste.

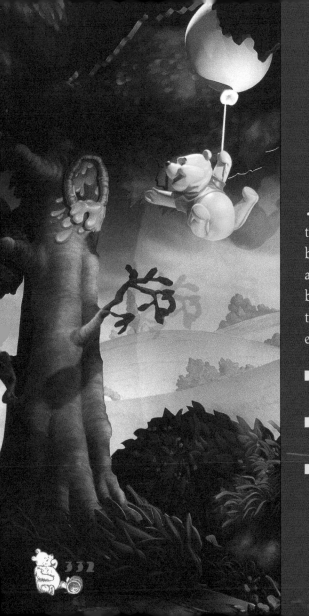

As Christopher Robin admits, the best moments in life are times of going along, listening to the things you cannot hear, and simply not bothering. Pooh agrees, and lives his life accordingly. But even the most lovable bear in all the world finds that there are those unexpected occasions when bothering is the only thing you can do:

- When your friend is out, and you must go on a fast thinking walk alone

- When you lose track of counting your honeypots

- When you acquire a piece of beehive where the bees are buzzing and not hunnying

"Bother!"

- When you trip and your pinecone flies into the river

- When another animal in the forest asks what you've been thinking, and in the process of asking, makes you forget

- When the wind causes you to bounce along on the sticks that used to be Eeyore's house

- When you can't think of what to get your friend for his birthday

- When you have unfull honeypots

- When you try to talk to (what you think is) a Tigger family member and he hops away (because he's really a frog)

- When you wake up sleeping bees

- When your stomach growls and your honeypots are empty

- When Christopher Robin isn't where he should be and wasn't where you were and seems not to be anywhere

- When you can't help Piglet be less afraid

- When you discover there is no way out and you shall have to stay in

- When Rabbit's come and gone so quickly you're not sure whether to say "hello" or "good-bye"

- When getting bounced into an entire pile of honeypots (but then again, that's not so bad, after all)

Celebrating Pooh!

When a bear has so many admirers, it comes as no surprise that he should be the focal point of many festive gatherings. While libraries from Iowa City, Iowa, to Boulder, Colorado, observed Pooh's seventy-fifth birthday in 2001, thousands in England trekked to Ashdown Forest, the inspiration for A. A. Milne's Hundred-Acre Wood. Since 1984, the British Rotary Club of Sinodun and Royal National Lifeboat Institution have held annual Pooh Sticks World Championships. And at Pembroke College in Oxford, the Winnie-the-Pooh Society meets for annual events and "expotitions," including a special Pooh Awareness Week. Here's a peek at how others continue to celebrate the Silly Old Bear:

■ Ever since the United Nations designated Winnie the Pooh as the world's Friendship Ambassador in 1997, The Walt Disney Company has celebrated Pooh Friendship Day festivals in France, Mexico, Canada, Japan, Australia, and the United States. Pooh's honorary status has made him the perfect candidate to celebrate the spirit of National Friendship Day every August, an event that was first introduced by Joyce C. Hall in 1919 to remember Samuel Johnson's advice to "keep one's friendships in constant repair." Past Pooh Friendship Day events have included character tours, stage entertainment, Pooh-themed activities, and adventures in re-created Hundred-Acre Woods.

■ The Alpha Tau Epsilon chapter of Delaware County Community College in Media, Pennsylvania, started "The Winnie the Pooh Challenge." Their goal: to inspire children to read. Chapter members traveled nearly 1,000 miles to share their love of Pooh. One chapter member dressed up as Winnie the Pooh as the troop visited hospitals and schools to read and act out the stories with children.

■ Every August, parades and music fill the streets of White River, Canada, the original home of Winnie, the famous black bear cub. Pooh fans of all ages gather for Winnie's Hometown Festival, which includes Pooh Sticks races, games, dancing, food, crafts, and live entertainment. The tradition started in 1988 to commemorate Lieutenant Harry Colebourn's purchase of Winnie from a local trapper in 1914.

Top right: Friendship Day 1998: Disney recording artist Marco Marinangeli with Tigger; above right: First Lady of the United Nations Nane Annan (right) and Kathy Lee Gifford (left) with Pooh.

You Never

According to Pooh, there are a few things of which you can never quite be certain:

Can Tell With . . .

- Heffalumps
- Bees
- Paw marks
- Honeypots
- Tiggers
- Piglets
- Rabbits
- Owls
- Bears

Sweet Dreams

Nighttime should be for slumbering in the land of dreams, but when a blustery day turns into a blustery night, or if there are lots of spookables about, dreams have a way of turning into nightmares. And for certain creatures in the Hundred-Acre Wood, some nightmares have a very real way of stealing honey. To ensure a restful sleep and still have a cupboard full of honey in the morning, here are some tips for conquering heffalumps and woozles that go bump in the night:

- Keep a popgun handy.

- Guard your honeypots.

- Avoid having late-night visitors who try to eat your honey and then say it's only fit for heffalumps and woozles.

- It may be helpful to hum a soothing sort of song.

- Heffalumps and woozles usually come through the windows, so be sure the bolts are secured.

- If you try to be kind to heffalumps, you may find that you'll be fresh out of honey in the morning.

- Check your honey cupboard frequently.

- If you are a very small animal like Piglet, don't spend time wondering if heffalumps like pigs, or, if they do, what sorts of pigs they might like.

- If you are a very small animal, it may be helpful to hide under the covers or in extreme cases, under the bed.

- If you have trouble sleeping, try counting sheep. Do *not* count heffalumps.

A Pooh Century

For nearly one hundred years, Winnie the Pooh and his friends have infiltrated the hearts, minds, and imaginations of generations of worldwide fans. Here's a peek at some of the highlights that have made Pooh the bear he is today:

1879 Ernest H. Shepard born

1882 Alan A. Milne born

1901 Walter Elias Disney born

1907 Wooden bridge built in Ashdown Forest, later to be known as Poohsticks Bridge

1913 *Punch* magazine publishes E. H. Shepard's illustration of Growler, the bear after which he later models Winnie the Pooh

1914 Lieutenant Harry Colebourn purchases a female American black bear from a Canadian trapper. Colebourn names her Winnipeg, after his hometown.

1920 Christopher Robin Milne born

1921 For his first birthday, Christopher Robin receives a stuffed teddy bear, purchased from Harrods in London

1921 For Christmas, Christopher Robin receives a stuffed donkey he names Eeyore

1924 Christopher Robin visits the London Zoo and becomes fascinated with a friendly American black bear named Winnipeg, or Winnie for short

1924 First appearance of Winnie the Pooh in *When We Were Very Young*

1925 On December 24, the London Evening News publishes *In Which We Are Introduced to Winnie-the-Pooh and Some Bees and the Stories Begin*. BBC radio broadcasts the story the following day.

1926 A. A. Milne's *Winnie-the-Pooh* published

1927 A. A. Milne's *Now We Are Six* published

1928 A. A. Milne's *The House at Pooh Corner* published

1947 E. P. Dutton Publishing Company president Elliott Macrae visits A. A. Milne and sees Christopher Robin's original toys that inspired the Winnie the Pooh stories. Macrae arranges for the toys to tour the United States. Milne later gives them to his American publisher.

1956 E. P. Dutton displays the original Pooh, Piglet, Eeyore, Tigger, and Kanga at the publisher's New York office

1956 A. A. Milne dies

1960 Latin translation of *Winnie the Pooh*, *Winnie Ille Pu*, makes *The New York Times* best-seller list for twenty weeks

1961 Walt Disney acquires the rights to produce films based on A. A. Milne's stories

1966 Premiere of Walt Disney featurette, *Winnie the Pooh and the Honey Tree*

1966 Walt Disney dies

1968 The Walt Disney Company wins Academy Award for Cartoon Short Subject, *Winnie the Pooh and the Blustery Day*

1969 The original Pooh and friends fly as VIPs on the Concorde to London for a special exhibit at the Victoria and Albert Museum commemorating E. H. Shepard's 90th birthday

1973 Color edition of A. A. Milne's *Winnie-the-Pooh* published

1976 The original Pooh and friends make another trip to England to celebrate the 50th anniversary of Milne's *Winnie-the-Pooh*, published by Methuen & Company

1976 World premiere of *Bother! A Selection From the Complete Works of Winnie-the-Pooh*, the internationally acclaimed one-man stage show performed by English actor Peter Dennis

1976 E. H. Shepard dies

1977 Theatrical release of *The Many Adventures of Winnie the Pooh*, which integrates Disney's first three Pooh featurettes and newly animated linking sequences

1979 Christopher Milne attends the unveiling ceremony of the commemorative bronze statue of Winnie, the American black bear who lived for twenty years at the London Zoo

1981 Christopher Milne unveils a bronze plaque in honor of his father A. A. Milne and E. H. Shepard at Ashdown Forest

1983 Premiere of *Winnie the Pooh and a Day for Eeyore*

1983 *Welcome to Pooh Corner* debuts on television on the Disney Channel

1987 The original Pooh, Kanga, Piglet, Eeyore, and Tigger stuffed animals take up permanent residence at the Donnell branch of the New York Public Library

1988 Professional conservationists treat, vacuum, and fix Christopher Robin's original dolls

1995 *Entertainment Weekly* names Pooh to its "In" list

1996 Christopher Robin Milne dies

1997 United Nations designates Winnie the Pooh as Honorary Ambassador of Friendship to the world's children

1998 British Member of Parliament Gwyneth Dunwoody stirs an international debate about whether the original Pooh and friends should return to England. The animals stay in New York.

1998 New York City Mayor Rudolph W. Giuliani proclaims May 4 Winnie the Pooh Day

1998 Winnie the Pooh appears in Disneyland Paris in a twenty-minute stage show in the Castle Stage Theater

1999 The Many Adventures of Winnie the Pooh attraction opens at Walt Disney World in Orlando, Florida

1999 In August, the East Sussex County Council appeals to Disney and the Countryside Agency to help save Poohsticks Bridge in Ashdown Forest, which has become worn out from all the Pooh fans' visiting the site

1999 Poohsticks Bridge receives necessary funding to build a replacement. The bridge closes to the public in September, and construction takes place the following month.

2000 In January, the new Poohsticks Bridge opens to the public

2000 Premiere of full length animated feature *The Tigger Movie*

2000 Pooh's Hunny Hunt attraction opens at Tokyo Disneyland

2001 *The Book of Pooh* airs on Disney Channel

2001 October 14, Pooh turns 75

The boy and the bear will always be together in this remarkable place called the Hundred-Acre Wood.

ACKNOWLEDGMENTS

Special thanks are due to Hugh Chitwood (Film Archivist, Slide Library-Walt Disney Imagineering), Dave Smith (Disney Archive Director), Denise R. Brown (Image Assets Administrator, WDI Art Library), Mike Jusko (Senior Art Archivist, WDI Art Library), Damon Whiteside (Executive Director, Marketing, Walt Disney Records), Lella F. Smith (Director, Walt Disney Feature Animation Research Library), Doug Engalla (Research Staff, Walt Disney Feature Animation Research Library), Fox Carney (Research Staff, Walt Disney Feature Animation Research Library), Tamara Khalaf (Database and Graphics Design, Walt Disney Feature Animation Research Library), Tina Santinelli-Lam (Creative Services Project Manager, Buena Vista Home Entertainment), David Penney (Creative Services Supervisor, Buena Vista Home Entertainment), Lia Murphy (Brand Marketing Director, Buena Vista Home Entertainment), Anne Moebes (Consultant, Disney Consumer Products), Ed Squair at the Walt Disney Photo Library, Duryan Bhagat (Global Managing Editor, Disney Publishing Worldwide), Jonathan Yaged (Director, Business Affairs, Disney Publishing Worldwide), Jack Anastasia (Synergy, Disney Publishing Worldwide), Tim Lewis (Disney Publishing Worldwide Digital Library), Teri Avanian (Disney Publishing Worldwide Digital Library), Tom Pniewski (Disney Publishing Worldwide Digital Library), Wendy Mogul (Disney Publishing Worldwide Digital Library), Natalie Farrey (Disney Publishing Worldwide Digital Library), Michael Horn (Executive Counsel Disney Corporate Administration), Michael Rola (Manager Animation Communications, Disney Television Productions), Patty Johnston (Manager Visual Communications, Disney Television Productions), and our Global Disney friends, including Sten Jorgensen, Laurence Bertel, Mira Wynant, Shiho Okada, Pia Knudsen, Stephanie Deusser, Dulce Lim, Paula Recabarren, and Rikke Lundbergh.

The producers also wish to acknowledge the following people for their indispensable contributions to this book: Kimberly Prince (ABC Photography), Peter Dennis, Lorne McKean, Lesley Milne, Liana C. Joyner (Editorial Manager, Photography & New Media ABC Television Network), Janelle Reynolds (Provincial Archive of Manitoba), the Lab Works, Jill Ratcliffe (Zoological Society of London), Sandra Powlette (British Library), Michael Boggan (British Library), Stephen Roper (British Library Reproductions–Western Manuscripts), Janice Swanson (Curtis Brown UK), Elizabeth Stevens (Curtis Brown UK), Jan Ramage (White River Heritage Museum), Janice Olsen (The University of Texas at Austin), Sherry White (Hobby House Press), Lisa Zuckerman (Hobby House Press), David Yanciw (www.bigthings.ca), Chris Donahue (Executive Director–Humanitas Prize), Brigitte Istim (*Punch* Cartoon Library & Archive), Joan Borsten Vidov (Jove Film), Fiodor Khitruk, Susan Hitches (Egmont Books Ltd.), Robert J. Sherman, David Yanciw, Carol J. Smith, Gerald Kornelsen, Anne Thwaite, Bill Sanderson, Dan Rogala, Gene Mann, Anna Sollovyev, Mike Ridley (Managing Director of Pooh Corner Limited), Peter Holle (President, Frontier Centre for Public Policy), Howard Peterson, Jeanne Lamb (Director of Central Children's Room, Donnell Library Center, New York Public Library), and Catherine Skrzypek (Senior Children's Librarian, Central Library, Brooklyn Public Library).

CAPTIONS & CREDITS

ART CAPTIONS

ART CREDITS

BIBLIOGRAPHY
BOOKS

Allen. Roger E. *Winnie-the-Pooh on Management: in Which a Very Important Bear and his friends are introduced to a Very Important Subject*. New York: Dutton, 1994.

Birnbaum's Disneyland 2002. New York: Disney Editions, 2001.

Birnbaum's Walt Disney World 2002. New York: Disney Editions, 2001.

Birnbaum's Walt Disney World for Kids by Kids 2002. New York: Disney Editions, 2001.

Canemaker, John. *Walt Disney's Nine Old Men & The Art of Animation*. New York: Disney Editions, 2001.

Cotter, Bill. *The Wonderful World of Disney Television: A Complete History*. New York: Hyperion, 1997.

Disney's Celebrate the Year with Winnie the Pooh: A Disney Holiday Treasury. New York: Disney Press, 1999.

Eeyore's Gloomy Little Instruction Book. Inspired by A. A. Milne with decorations by Ernest H. Shepard. New York: Dutton, 1996.

Finch, Christopher. *Disney's Winnie the Pooh: A Celebration of the Silly Old Bear.* New York: Disney Editions, 2000.

Grant, John. *Encyclopedia of Walt Disney's Animated Characters: From Mickey Mouse to Hercules*. New York: Hyperion, 1998.

Hoff, Benjamin. *The Tao of Pooh*. New York: Penguin, 1983.

Many Adventures of Winnie the Pooh, The: A Classic Disney Treasury. New York: Disney Press, 1995.

Melrose, A. R. *The Pooh Dictionary: The Complete Guide to the Words of Pooh & All the Animals in the Forest*. With decorations by Ernest H. Shepard. New York: Dutton Books, 1995.

Milne, A. A. *The House at Pooh Corner*. Decorations by Ernest H. Shepard. New York: E. P. Dutton, 1928.

Milne, A. A. *Winnie-the-Pooh: The Color Edition*. Decorations by Ernest H. Shepard. New York: Dutton, 1991.

Milne, Christopher. *Beyond the World of Pooh: Selections from the Memoirs of Christopher Milne*. Edited by A. R. Melrose. New York: Dutton, 1998.

Pooh's Little Instruction Book. Inspired by A. A. Milne with decorations by Ernest H. Shepard. New York: Dutton, 1995.

Smith, Carol J. *Identification & Price Guide to Winnie the Pooh Collectibles*. Grantsville, Md: Hobby House Press, Inc., 1994.

Smith, Carol J. *Identification & Price Guide to Winnie the Pooh Collectibles II*. Grantsville, Md: Hobby House Press, Inc., 1996.

Smith, Dave, and Steven Clark. *Disney: The First 100 Years*. New York: Hyperion, 1999.

Smith, Dave. *Disney A to Z: The Updated Official Encyclopedia*. New York: Hyperion, 1998.

Thwaite, Ann. *The Brilliant Career of Winnie-the-Pooh: The Definitive History of the Best Bear in All the World*. New York: Dutton Children's Books, 1992.

Thwaite, Ann. *A. A. Milne: The Man Behind Winnie-the-Pooh*. New York: Random House, 1990.

Walt Disney's The Many Adventures of Winnie the

Pooh: A Classic Disney Treasury. New York: Disney Press, 1994.

PERIODICALS

"Exotic New Pooh." *Disney Magazine*, Winter 2000-2001.

Fanning, Jim. "70 Years in the Hundred Acre Wood." *Disney Magazine*, Winter 1994.

Sastrowardoyo, Rahadyan. "Pooh's New Adventures, in a 100-Gigabyte Wood." *The New York Times*, January 21, 2001.

Smith, Liz. "The Big Picture." *Disney Magazine*, Spring 2000.

Tracy, Joe. "A Behind the Scenes Look at *The Tigger Movie*." www.animationartist.com

WEB SITES

The Ashdown Forest Guide — Online:
www.ashdownforest.co.uk
The Bunraku:
http://osaka.yomiuri.co.jp/bunraku/english
DCW! Disney Comics Worldwide:
www.wolfstad.com/dcw/
Disney Online: http://disney.go.com
The Internet Movie Database: www.imdb.com
The Literary World of Winnie the Pooh:
www.bright.net/~kbaumle/index.html
National Honey Board: www.nhb.org
The New York Public Library: www.nypl.org
Pooh Corner: www.pooh-corner.com
Sherman Music: www.shermanmusic.com
Sussex Top Attractions: www.sussextourism.org.uk
Teddy Bear and Friends: teddybearandfriends.com
Voice Chasers: www.voicechasers.org
Winnie the Pooh: www.just-pooh.com/home.html

ANSWERS TO GAMES

170-171 Owl's Cryptic Cryptograms:

1. PLES RING IF AN RNSER IS REQIRD
2. WOL
3. PLEZ CNOKE IF AN RNSR IS NOT REQID
4. HIPY PAPY BTHUTHDTH THUTHDA BTHUTHDY
5. A BEAR WEDGED IN GREAT TIGHTNESS
6. THE WOLERY
7. HE CAN SPELL TUESDAY

318–319 Musical Chairs:

1. G, 2. I, 3. E, 4. A, 5. H, 6. B, 7. C, 8. D, 9. F

248-249 What's the Score, Honey?

1. Winnie the Pooh
2. Up, Down, and Touch the Ground
3. Rumbly in My Tumbly
4. Little Black Rain Cloud
5. Mind Over Matter
6. A Rather Blustery Day
7. The Wonderful Thing About Tiggers
8. The Rain, Rain, Rain Came Down, Down, Down
9. Heffalumps and Woozles
10. Hip Hip Pooh-Ray

276–277 Christopher Robin's Crossword:

Across: 2. Sanders, 8. Balloon, 9. Jagular, 10. Mild zephyr, 11. Tail

Down: 1. Scarf, 3. Ambush, 4. Bounce, 5. Woozle, 6. Sandy pit, 7. Rain

The End